NEW VANGUARD 230

IMPERIAL ROMAN WARSHIPS 27 BC–193 AD

RAFFAELE D'AMATO   ILLUSTRATED BY GIUSEPPE RAVA

First published in Great Britain in 2016 by Osprey Publishing,
Kemp House, Chawley Park, Cumnor Hill, Oxford OX2 9PH, UK
29 Earlsfort Terrace, Dublin 2, Ireland
1385 Broadway, 5th Floor, New York, NY 10018, USA

Osprey Publishing, part of Bloomsbury Publishing Plc

© 2016 Osprey Publishing – Email: info@ospreypublishing.com

All rights reserved. Apart from any fair dealing for the purpose of private study, research, criticism or review, as permitted under the Copyright, Designs and Patents Act, 1988, no part of this publication may be reproduced, stored in a retrieval system, or transmitted in any form or by any means, electronic, electrical, chemical, mechanical, optical, photocopying, recording or otherwise, without the prior written permission of the copyright owner. Enquiries should be addressed to the Publishers.

A CIP catalogue record for this book is available from the British Library.

Print ISBN: 978 1 4728 1089 2
PDF eBook ISBN: 978 1 4728 1090 8
ePub eBook ISBN: 978 1 4728 1091 5

Index by Sharon Redmayne
Typeset in Sabon and Myriad Pro
Originated by PDQ Media, Bungay, UK
Printed and bound in Great Britain

Transferred to digital print on demand 2021

Osprey Publishing supports the Woodland Trust, the UK's leading woodland conservation charity. Between 2014 and 2018 our donations were spent on their Centenary Woods project in the UK.

www.ospreypublishing.com

Title page image: A detail from a wall painting from the same temple as the Isis fresco, showing the stern of another warship. The ship is entering a harbour, its deck packed with soldiers. Note the twin steering oars. Reconstruction on plate H. (Naples, National Archaeological Museum, author's photograph, courtesy of the museum)

DEDICATION
In Memoriam Géza Alföldy

ACKNOWLEDGEMENTS
A great number of people, museums, and institutions have contributed to this book. A very special thanks must be given to Admiral Domenico Carro, who again shared with me his precious knowledge of the Roman Navy, enriching the book with wonderful illustrations. Prof. Livio Zerbini of Ferrara University has been as always invaluable in helping to obtain from different museums and institutions permission to see and photograph the relevant material.

The material related to the Musei Capitolini, the Antiquarium of the Palatino and the Museo Nazionale di Palazzo Massimo has been obtained thanks to D.ssa Marina Mattei, curator of the Musei Capitolini and director of the Excavations of the Area Sacra di Largo Argentina, and thanks to the courtesy of D.ssa Rita Paris, director of the Museo Nazionale Romano. I would also like to thank Dr. Andrea Camilli who allowed me to publish precious material from the wonderful site of San Rossore.

The finds of Comacchio, have been published thanks only to the invaluable help and collaboration of Dr. Fede Berti of the Museo Archeologico of Ferrara, to whom I would like to express all my gratitude for her assistance in the field. Dr.ssa Giuseppina Ghini has been so kind in allowing me to publish material from the new museum of the Nemi ship, and allowing me to visit and inspect the material.

For the photographic credits I would like to thank the following museums and institutions: the Museo Archeologico Nazionale of Aquileia; the Museo Archeologico Nazionale di Napoli; the Soprintendenza Archeologica di Pompeii, Herculaneum and Stabia; the Museo di Ostia Antica; the Museo della civiltà Romana; the British Museum; the Musée Carnavalet; and the Antikenmuseum der Universitaet Leipzig.

Special thanks must be given also for the always precious assistance and inestimable help in collecting the photographic material, searching the sources, preparing the drawings, patiently assisting in my various travels and in many other numerous activities, to Dr. Andrea Salimbeti and Dr. Massimo Bizzarri. Last but not least, I am deeply grateful to my dear friend and illustrator, Giuseppe Rava, who has provided a new and splendid set of illustrations on the Imperial Roman Navy.

GLOSSARY

Antennae: pennons

àphlaston (aplustre): the raising of the stern

Carina: keel

Costae: the ribs of the ship

Epotis, επωτις: thick beam at the forward end of an outrigger or oarbox, cathead. More in detail, the ear-like projection on each side of the bow of the oared warship formed by a beam lying athwartships at the forward end of the oarboxes so to protect them from damage in bow to bow collision.

Foredeck: the deck forward of the *epotis*, and aft of the stempost

Gubernaculum: rudder

Harmoniai: joints made of mortises and tenons to fasten the ribs and planks to the hull of the ship

Louvre: protected ventilation course

Malo: mast

Navis, Naves: ship, ships

Navita: helmsman

Parasimon, παρασημον: panel on each side of the bow of a warship facing half-front containing a symbol or figure illustrating the ship's name

Parexeiresia, παρεξειρεσια: outriggers, auxiliary fittings for the oars, small arches on the external structure of the hull on which the oars of the *traniti* found their foothold

Parodos: gangway

Proembolion: fore ram or subsidiary ram that projects forwards above the waterline ram, whose purpose is to prevent entanglement or damage to the ship's superstructure at the bow, during ramstrikes

Puppis: stern

Rostrum: ram

Rudentes: ropes

skinì: stern shelter

Spina, tropis: keel

Stempost: the curved timber rising from the keel in the bow and culminating in an ornament or figure-head

Stolos: ornament of the prow

Stylis: a pole, generally fitted with a short crosspiece, which was set up across the *aplustre* and bore the device of the ship, usually the flag

Thalamites: the lowermost oarsmen on a three-level warship

Thranites: rowers in the topmost reme in a multireme warship

Vela: sail

Wale: assemblage end to end of thick and broad planks along a ship's side and worked into the hull planking.

Zygites: middle oarsmen on a three-level warship

CONTENTS

INTRODUCTION   4

THE ROMAN NAVY IN THE EARLY EMPIRE   4
- The Year of the Four Emperors

EMPLOYMENT OF THE FLEET IN CONQUEST WARS
- The Conquest of Dacia (101–106 AD)
- The Roman fleet in the *Bellum Germanicum et Sarmaticum* (166–180 AD)
- The naval *blitzkrieg* of Septimius Severus (197 AD)

THE ORGANIZATION OF THE IMPERIAL ROMAN NAVY   15
- The Roman fleets of *Classis* (Ravenna) and Misenum
- The Provincial Fleets

IMPERIAL ROMAN WARSHIPS AND BOATS   24
- The evolution of the *Biremes*
- The evolution of the *Triremes*
- The evolution of the *Quadriremes* and *Quinquiremes*
- The *Hexeris* or *Six* and the *Deceris*
- The *Actuaria* and the *Oneraria*
- Structure and Construction
- Armament and Decoration

FIGHTING ON THE SEA: ROMAN NAVAL TACTICS IN THE EARLY EMPIRE   43

BIBLIOGRAPHY   46

INDEX   48

IMPERIAL ROMAN WARSHIPS 27 BC–193 AD

Fresco, 54–68 AD, Odysseus' ship. In this fresco fragment, Odysseus' ship is a cataphract Roman warship, with parapets for the crew and closed boxes for the oarsmen. Note the yellow colours of the oars and the white prow (*prora*). (British Museum, London, photograph courtesy of Domenico Carro)

INTRODUCTION

The Roman Empire was not only built by the strength of the legions, but also by a navy that was one of the most powerful maritime forces ever to have existed. It was only the existence of Rome's fleet that secured its trade routes and maintained communications within the huge Empire. At the height of its power the Roman Navy employed tens of thousands of sailors, marines and craftsmen, coming from every corner of the three continents under the rule of the Caesars.

This powerful navy allowed the Empire to maintain naval supremacy throughout Europe, North Africa and Western Asia for the first two centuries of its existence. Therefore Imperial Rome poured a great deal of manpower, money and resources into its navies, perfecting the use of warships not only at sea, but also on the great rivers of Europe. This meant that large quantities of soldiers, goods and materials could be transported by river, which was fundamental to the success of the great military operations in Germania and Dacia. As correctly noted by Pitassi, water was one of the key elements that decided how the Empire would grow and expand.

The number of Roman shipwreck finds in recent years has greatly increased archaeologists' knowledge of Roman shipbuilding techniques, and of the rich material culture of the ships' crews. Despite the fact that no real Roman warship has been identified or made public, the archaeological information gathered from other Roman shipwrecks, coupled with the very rich iconography of the period, has allowed us to reconstruct the key warship types of this glorious age of Imperial Roman power.

THE ROMAN NAVY IN THE EARLY EMPIRE

In 31 BC, in the aftermath of Actium,[1] Octavian – now Emperor Augustus – commanded not only the combined legions of his own and Mark Antony's armies, but also a number of strong naval formations. The fleet that had won

---

[1] For information on the earlier Roman navy, see NVG 225: *Republican Roman Warships 509–27 BC* by the same author

Warships on the Isis fresco, Pompeii, first century AD. The two ships advancing under oar on the fresco in the Temple of Isis show half of the bow and the port side. One of the ships (left) has a forward curving (Carthaginian style) stempost with an *àkrostolion* similar to the bird's head visible on ancient Carthaginian coins. This, and the more 'Roman' appearance of the second ship (right), has led Morrison to believe the scene might be a historical representation of the Punic Wars. The main deck of both ships is packed with marines armed with shields and spears. (Naples, National Archaeological Museum, inv. LSRS 35b, SSAW 133,973, author's photograph, courtesy of the museum)

the decisive victory numbered about 400 ships. This victorious fleet was in the Mediterranean along with the captured ships and crews of former enemies, especially those of Sextus Pompeius, and this included around 700 ships of all kinds. In the northern seas the formations of Julius Caesar were still operating along the coasts of Gaul. The fleets that sailed along the Rhine and to the east, in the Pontus Euxinus, were still those created by Pompey. All the ships that had belonged to Antony were positioned in the Levant, as it seems that, in both cases, most of the ships had been moved from their bases to reinforce Augustus' fleet at Actium.

Augustus used these ships as the basis of a new Roman standing navy, on the model of the navies of the Hellenistic Kingdoms. He wanted to create a permanent naval force with its own permanent bases; for the fleet's importance had been clearly demonstrated during the war against Sextus Pompeius and in the final clash with Antony and Cleopatra. According to the *Monumentum Ancyranum* (*Res Gestae Divi Augusti*, 3), of the 600 ships captured from Augustus during the civil wars, some were burned, but 300 of them – mainly the ones taken from Cleopatra at Actium – formed the bulk of the fleet of *Forum Julii*, the new military harbour built in the south of Gaul, which was destined to control the coasts of Spain and Gaul. Beside the *Forum Julii*, Augustus created two stronger military harbours for two Praetorian Fleets (*Classes Praetoriae*): one at Misenum (*Classis Misenensis*), at the northern end of the Bay of Naples, to cover the south-west of the Mediterraenan Sea, and the second at Ravenna (*Classis Ravennatis*), to control the Adriatic. The choice of the two locations was due merely to strategic needs: to have large and safe harbours that possessed good land communications.

Ravenna was perfectly situated to control the whole of the Adriatic, and especially to watch for possible piratical activity on the Dalmatian coast; and from there the conquest of Illyricum could be supplied and reinforced. The Misenum fleet was best placed to intercept any seaborne attack from Africa or the East against Rome. A certain number of outposts were also mantained, such as Ostia, the harbour of Rome.

From the moment that Augustus consolidated his power, the entire Mediterranean was a Roman-controlled sea, but during the Imperial age this did not exclude the occasional outbreak of piracy. In this time, the Mediterranean also saw Roman fleets engaging in combat during the civil wars.

With the consolidation of the Empire, the Romans now controlled territory bordering the Atlantic as well as rivers such as the Rhine, the Danube and the Nile. *Classes* or fleets became a standard part of the armed forces. Their main duties were to protect maritime trade, maintain Imperial

CHRONOLOGY

31–30 BC	After the battle of Actium, the young Gaius Julius Caesar Octavianus (Emperor Augustus) is the sole master of the *Res Publica*. Augustus makes new arrangements for the Roman fleets, stationing a fleet at Misenum (in the Bay of Naples) and another at Ravenna (on the Adriatic coast), to defend the Upper and Lower seas (Suetonius, *Aug.*, 49)
29 BC	*Naumachia* (gladiatorial naval battle) organised by Augustus; Agrippa establishes the headquarters of the fleet at *Portum Argonautorum*, inside the Campus Martius at Rome
26 BC	Naval campaign of Aelius Gallus, *Praefectus Aegypti* (Prefect of Egypt), against the Arabian Sabei, with 80 warships and 130 *onerariae* of the *Classis Arabica*
25 BC	Naval and land operations of Gaius Petronius, the new Egyptian Prefect, against the Ethiopians (the Meroites, Strabo, 17,1,54)
16 BC	Campaigns of Drusus and Tiberius on the upper and lower Danube; creation of the first nucleus of the later *Classis Pannonica* and *Classis Moesica*
14 BC	Agrippa sails east with the fleet to visit the Provincia and meets Herod the Great (Josephus, *Jewish Antiquities*, XVI, 2, 1)
12 BC	Creation of the first nucleus of the future *Classis Germanica* by Drusus; campaigns and explorations by Drusus from the lower Rhine to the North Sea; the ships of the *Bructeri*, a Germanic tribe, are destroyed by the Roman fleet; the Romans create *Provincia Germanica*
4 AD	Tiberius' fleet sails up the Albis (now the Elba) river, the Roman ships reach Norway
9 AD	After the disaster of Teutoburgus, the Roman fleet, with 15,000 men of the *Classes Praetoriae* and 15,000 of the *Classis Germanica*, is stationed in permanent bases along the Rhine
16 AD	A fleet of 1,000 ships is built by Germanicus (Tacitus, *Annales*., II, 6) for the operations in Germany on the Rhine; the Roman fleet sails from the mouth of the Rhine (in the modern Netherlands) eastward as far as the lands of the Cimbri (*Res Gestae Divi Augusti*, 26); a victorious Roman land and naval campaign is fought against the Dacians of the *Classis Moesica* on the lower Danube
18–19 AD	The fleet escorts Germanicus in the east and, later, his body at his State funeral (Tacitus, *Annales*, II, 53–9; III, 1)
24 AD	The *Classis Ravennatis* is engaged in the repression of revolts at Brundisium (modern Brindisi); from 24 AD, the fleet is stationed here on a permanent basis in order to control the Adriatic Sea
28 AD	Frisian insurrection; the Roman fleet is concentrated on the Rhine; Caius Poppeus Sabinus is commander of the *Classis Moesica* (on the Danube)
36 AD	The *Classis Ravennatis* is sent by Emperor Tiberius in Cilicia to crush a new attempt at piracy by the inhabitants
39 AD	Naval and land raids by Caius Caligula in Germania
41–42 AD	The revolt in Mauretania (in modern Algeria) is crushed by Claudius who creates the *Mauretania Caesariensis*, with its capital Colonia Claudia Caesarea (modern Cherchell) elevated to the status of military harbour
43 AD	Invasion of Britannia and creation of the powerful *Classis Britannica*; 300 *onerariae*, escorted by the *Classes Germanica* and *Britannica*, transport the 40,000 men of the invasion force
45 AD	The *Classis Moesica* restores a king loyal to Roman interests in the Kingdom of the Pontus Euxinus (the Black Sea)
46 AD	Definitive annexation of Thracia and creation of the *Classis Perinthia*
47 AD	The historian Tacitus is with the fleet in Scandinavia
50 AD	The rebellious Welsh tribes of Siluri are attacked by the Roman fleet
52 AD	The *Classis Germanica* destroys a small fleet of the rebellious Chauci; Roman ships operate on the southwestern coasts of Britannia
54 AD	Inauguration of Portus, the harbour of Rome, in the presence of the Emperor Nero
62 AD	Creation of the *Classis Pontica* for Corbulo's operations against the Parthians on the Pontus Euxinus
66 AD	Fast Roman liburns (*liburnicae*) escort the informer Antistius Sosianus to Rome (Tacitus, *Annales*, XVI, 14)
67 AD	The *Classis Alexandrina* support the Roman army of Vespasianus in the repression of the Jewish Revolt
68 AD	Nero unsuccessfully asks for the help of the naval squadron of Ostia to escape to Egypt; the naval base of *Forum Julii* (at modern Frejus) is abandoned with only with a small detachment of the *Classis Misenensis* left; the *classes* of the Rhine and Italy are involved in the civil war; the provincial fleets do not take part in the civil war, but stay inactive under the orders of the local governors
69 AD	During the Year of the Four Emperors, a fleet of Emperor Otho sets sail in February, to raid the southern coast of Gaul and delay the advance of Valens, legatus of the Emperor Vitellius; the rebellion of Anicetus, whose fleet conquers Trabzon (on the Black Sea in

Liburna, detail of the Isis fresco, Pompeii, first century AD. (Naples, National Archaeological Museum, author's photograph, courtesy of the museum)

A relief shaped like the ram of a ship, representing the triumphant Agrippa, last quarter of the first century BC. In this relief, typical of the *Rostrum* shape celebrating the naval victories, Agrippa, victor of Actium, is celebrated, crowned by a winged victory. (Antikenmuseum der Universitaet Leipzig, inv. 99059, author's photograph, courtesy of the museum)

	modern Turkey), is put down by the *Legatus* Geminus with land and naval forces; revolt of Gaius Julius Civilis
69 AD, September	Cornelius Fuscus, *legatus* of Vespasian, is the new commander of the *Classis Ravennatis*; the old commander, Bassus, is arrested and brought to Atria on board a warship; the Vitellian loyalists capture three galleys of the same *Classis* on the river Po, killing all marines and sailors; a combined action of the *Classis Ravennatis* and the *Classis* of Forum Julii put to an end the resistance of Valens, last general of Vitellius; in Germany, after the failed double attempt of Civilis to conquest *Vetera*, the rest of the *Classis Germanica* loyal to Rome is stationed in *Confluentes* (Koblenz)
69 AD, December	Clash between units of the *Classis Britannica* and the ships of Civilis on the western shores of the Rhine; the Roman ships are mainly destroyed; the Roman fleet on the Rhine is reorganized by Cerialis, and eventually Civilis surrenders
71 AD	Operations of the *Classis Britannica* in the North, under Cerialis, convey troops and supplies for the establishment of a new naval base, Petuaria (now in East Yorkshire)
78 AD	In the east the *Classis Pontica* stamps out the last vestiges of piracy in the *Pontus Euxinus*
79 AD	The *Classis Misenensis*, under Pliny the Elder, is engaged in helping refugees from the eruption of Vesuvius in Pompeii, Herculaneum and Stabia
80 AD	Advance of Agricola in Caledonia with the support of the fleet on both east and west coasts of Scotland; the Romans arrive in the Orcades (Orkney Islands)
82–85 AD	The ships of Agricola arrive on Ireland's coasts; naval and land offensive against the Caledonians on the river Tay; further operations in the area interrupted by the Dacian incursions on the Danube, cause serious losses to the *Classis Moesica*
89 AD	The *Classis Germanica* puts down the incursion of the Chatti, and receives from Emperor Domitianus the title of *Pia Fidelis*
101–106 AD	The fleets of the *Classis Moesica* and the *Classes Praetoriae* are engaged in the First and Second Dacian Wars under the Emperor Trajan
106 AD	Roman ships, probably of the *Classis Arabica*, operate in the Indian Ocean; the fleet is also involved in the military operations connected to the creation of the Provincia of Arabia by Trajan
117 AD	To put down the Jewish riots that were formenting in the Levant, Cyrene, Egypt and Judea, the Romans send units of the *Classis Misenensis* in the East, to help to restore order; disembarked sailors and soldiers escort the Emperor Trajan and negotiate with local leaders for the security of maritime routes
122 AD	The *Classis Germanica* ferries the Legio VI Victrix from the Rhine to Britannia, to Newcastle upon Tyne; in Egypt the Emperor Hadrian orders the *Classis Alexandrina* to launch a naval squadron in the Red Sea against piratical activity in the area
144–150 AD	Campaigns of Emperor Antoninus Pius against the Moors in North Africa and naval operations of the *Syriaca* and *Alexandrina* fleets
166 AD	Roman naval embassy sent to China by the Emperor, Marcus Aurelius
168 AD	Owing to the invasions of Quadi and Marcomanni, the *Classis Pontica* moves to Cyzicus from Trapezus, to stop any attempt by the Barbarians to cross into Asia
168–180 AD	The Roman fleets of the Danube are involved in the Marcomannic Wars of Emperor Marcus Aurelius
170–171 AD	The *Classis Misenensis* suppresses piratical activity of the tribes southwest of Mauritania
184 AD	The *Classis Britannica* ferries troops from Britannia, under their commander Lucius Artorius Castus, in Armorica, to suppress an uprising
192 AD	The *Classes Ravennatis* and *Misenensis* align themselves with Emperor Septimius Severus against Didius Julianus; the Italian fleets ferry his men to the Balkans, for the civil war against Pescennius Niger. Naval blockade and conquest of Byzantium by Septimius Severus
197 AD	The Fleet of Severus attacks and raids Ctesiphon on the river Euphrates

Roman cargo carrier *rostrata*, from the mosaic of the Guildes, c. 122 AD. Many ships among those represented in this famous mosaic are smaller versions of the bigger warships. The smallest ships were used by the army for exploratory duties, and were called *naves lusoriae*. (Ostia, in situ, photo courtesy of Domenico Carro)

These two ships show *triremes* of the *Misenensis* fleet, one of which may be a flagship. The two reliefs show stemposts and three levels of oars, but there are several differences between them. The ship without a flag recalls the ship of the Praeneste relief. By making the details of the ship larger, the artist is suggesting that it is a bigger ship. (Pozzuoli reliefs, 25 BC–25 AD, originals and cast from the Naples National Archaeological Museum, Museum, inv. LSRS 32a and b, SSAW 129, 131, B. 962,963 and from Museum of the Civiltà Romana, Roma. Author's and Domenico Carro's photos, courtesy of the museums)

communications and to transport, supply and support the army during military campaigns. During this period, in which the fleet was widely employed against the Germanic tribes in North Europe, the Roman fleet pushed to the Empire's furthest extent along the coasts of the North Sea, marred by great difficulties and shipwrecks due to the often treacherous weather conditions (Tacitus, *Annales* II 6–8, 23–24).

The Year of the Four Emperors

In addition to the campaigns in North Europe and the extensive deployment of the fleet in Claudius' 43 AD invasion of Britannia, the Roman fleets are also mentioned by historians as the protagonists of fierce clashes in the civil wars of 69 AD, the Year of the Four Emperors. With no serious maritime rivals in its home waters in the early Empire, the Roman navy saw little action in the Mediterranean except during these civil wars. The commanders of the fleets were not exempt from personal risks. During Vitellius' insurrection in that tumultuous year, the commander of the *Classis Germanica*, Julius Burdo, was threatened with death by his soldiers, and was saved only by the personal intervention of Vitellius.

Tacitus (Hist. 2, 12, 1) speaks expressly about the sea power of Emperor Otho, the second emperor of 69 AD, who was able to block the Adriatic Sea. Thanks to this maritime power, he dispatched a strong fleet of the *Classis Misenensis* to the southern coast of Gaul (*Gallia Narbonensis*), although the number of embarked troops (*Urbaniciani* and *Praetoriani*) and marines was relatively small. His aim was most likely to reach and conquer the important new military harbour of *Forum Julii* there. The fleet set sail from Ostia, and made its way up the western Italian coast. But strife between the commanders provoked a mutiny, and the appointed general, Aemilius Pacencis, was put in chains.

The new commander, Suedius Clemens, was unable to control the sailors and the troops. According to Tacitus, the fleet created havoc wherever it put in, even when it was still in Italian territory. The soldiers pillaged, murdered, sacked and burned the coasts in their four days of navigation towards Gaul; their victims had not expected this assault to come from the sea. When the fleet reached the tiny province of the Maritime Alps, the *Procurator*, Marius Maturus, tried to organize resistance, using a local militia of young men. But untrained and with no experience of war, these young people took flight

The 'Carthaginian' ship, detail from the Isis fresco of Pompeii, first century AD. The main deck of the ships here represented are packed with marines armed with shields and spears. This suggests that the scene probably represents a *Naumachia*, or a naval exercise, where one party is 'playing' the Carthaginians and the other the Romans. What is clear is that both ships are copied from contemporary warships at the time of painting, belonging to the category of the τριημιολίαι, according to Morrison, or to that of the *liburnae*, according to Pitassi. (Naples, National Archaeological Museum, inv. LSRS 35b, SSAW 133,973, author's photograph, courtesy of the museum)

when attacked. The rage of the marines and embarked soldiers turned on the citizens of Albintimilium (Ventimiglia). Tacitus, who reports the drama, was personally involved, because Agricola's mother, Tacitus' grandmother-in-law, was one of the victims, as brutal soldiers sacked her estate near Albintimilium. After having committed further atrocities, the fleet and the Othonians paused there, ready to attack westwards.

News of their approach found the ears of Valens, Vitellius' general in the area, who sent a strong armed force to intercept them. In the following battle, on a flat plain near the city, the ships were covering the left wings of the Otho's army, with their prows towards the coast, against the normal practice. The *Urbaniciani* were embarked as reserve forces on the ships. During the first clash, slingbolts and missiles from the Othonian front line and probably from the ships dispersed and put to flight the Treveran cavalrymen of Valens' army. A few days later, the counterattack of the Vitellians put to flight the Othonians and panicked the ships' crews: but the resistance of the Praetorians transformed the defeat to a stalemate, and both forces withdrew, the Othonian fleet returning to Albingaunum (Albenga). Here the maritime expedition ended.

The final and decisive battle of this stage of the civil war was the battle of Bedriacum, fought in northern Italy in April 69 AD, between the Vitellians and the Othonians. Here, Caecina, one of the Vitellian commanders, ordered his men to build a pontoon bridge across the river Po. The Vitellians probably used the rowing boats or barges of the local inhabitants. The ships were aligned with their prows pointing upstream, and were fastened together at bow and stern with heavy beams that carried the roadbed. They were

The 'Roman ship' from the Isis fresco. The ship shows a typical backward curving stempost in Roman style. Note the gap between the deck above and the bulwark towards the bow to allow for the placing of a gangplank when tied up at the quayside. (Naples, National Archaeological Museum, inv. LSRS 35b, SSAW 133,973, author's photograph, courtesy of the museum)

This detail of the Isis fresco shows *Liburnica biremis* of the *Misenensis* fleet. Note the blue colour (*venetus*) of the ships, quite typical of Roman warships. (Naples, National Archaeological Museum, author's photograph, courtesy of the museum)

anchored too, but the hawsers had enough play in them for the line not to break if the level of the river rose suddenly, as could happen in spring. The Othonians launched fire ships against the pontoon from the south bank, but they ignited prematurely because of a sudden change of the wind, and the crews had to jump overboard and swim for their lives. After the defeat, Otho killed himself and Vitellius was temporarily master of the Empire. Very soon the Eastern Legions proclaimed their commander, Titus Flavius Vespasianus, as Emperor. The *Classis Pontica* was concentrated at Byzantium, to support Mucianus, Vespasian's legate, who had left for Italy with the Syrian legions (Tacitus, *Histories*, II, 83).

Meanwhile, the Roman fleet of the Rhine, under the command of Cerialis, was involved in heavy clashes with the Batavi and the other Germanic rebels commanded by Civilis, who, exploiting the ongoing Roman civil war, had raised the Batavian revolt, and captured a substantial number of ships of *Classis Germanica*. After Cerialis' inspection tour of the camps that were being built for the legions' winter quarters, he was returning with the fleet when he was ambushed by Civilis' troops. Part of the German force threw the fleet into confusion, throwing grappling irons on board and dragging the boats away. The rebels dragged away his flagship, which was distinguished by a standard, and sailed off in broad daylight on the ships they had captured; they sailed the flagship up the Lippe as a gift to the Priestess Veleda, soul of the rebellion. Boosted by the victory, Civilis was seized with a desire to make a naval demonstration. The place chosen for the display was a small sea, at the point where the mouth of the Maas discharges the water of the Rhine into the ocean. His purpose was to frighten away the convoys of supplies that were coming from Gaul. Cerialis drew up his fleet, which, although inferior in numbers, was superior in having more experienced rowers, more skilful pilots and larger ships. The stream was helping the Roman ships, while their opponents were instead enjoying a favourable wind; so they sailed past each other and separated, after trying some shots with light missiles. Civilis dared attempt nothing further, but withdrew across the Rhine; later Cerialis devastated the island of the Batavians.

In Italy, after the victorious battle of Cremona, and also thanks to the decisive intervention of the *Classis Ravennatis*, which was patrolling the Adriatic Sea on his behalf, Vespasianus emerged as the new emperor of the Roman *Res Publica*. The *Classis Misenensis* passed to the command of the new Emperor; notwithstanding six ships of this fleet were sunk by the Vitellians in a last desperate fight at Terracina.

After the advent of the Flavian dynasty the fleet played an even bigger role in sustaining Imperial power. It was active in the military operations against the Dacians under the Emperor Domitian and then during the victorious wars of Trajan in Dacia and Mesopotamia. During the Marcomannic War the fleet was crucial to the final victory of Marcus Aurelius. Stationed at the important centres Taurunum, Carnuntum and Brigetio, the fleet could resupply the army along the river Danube. Septmius Severus, in his fight for the Imperial throne, fought a very difficult naval battle against the Byzantines, who supported his rival Pescennius Niger (Dio Cassius, LXXV). His fleet closed in to blockade the city, but Byzantium was well defended.

The Byzantines had a powerful fleet of 500 ships, most of them with one bank of oars (*moneres*), but some with two (*dikrota*), and all equipped with beaks (*emboloi*). Some of them were provided with rudders at both ends, at the prow as well as the stern, and had a double complement of helmsmen and sailors, in order that they might both attack and retire without turning round and might outmanoeuvre their opponents both in advancing and in retreating. This was a local fleet built by the inhabitants of the city with the booty they took from other ships and merchants during the disorders following the civil

Liburnae of the *Misenensis* fleet in the Isis fresco. Note again the blue colour (*venetus*) of both ships and the very well preserved rostrum of the vessel on the right. (Naples, National Archaeological Museum, author's photograph, courtesy of the museum)

This detail of the Isis fresco shows a *liburnian* of the *Misenensis* fleet. The deck above (*katastroma*) is edged with a low bulwark to which shields are attached to provide protection. Note the stem with elaborate carving, which recalls some of the stemposts of the ships on the monumental arch of Arausius (nowadays Orange, France). (Naples, National Archaeological Museum, author's photograph, courtesy of the museum)

Liburnica biremis of the *Misenensis Fleet*, from another of the eight naval scenes in the Temple of Isis. All the details of the cataphract ship are visible, including the unusual raised stempost, which ends with what could be the head of a swan. (Naples, National Archaeological Museum, author's photograph, courtesy of the museum)

wars. Moreover, the city was well fortified and defended by heavy artillery on the towers and chains closing its harbours. However, using his ships, Severus was able to blockade supplies to the city; and when some citizens tried to escape in their ships, the Romans attacked and sank them, collecting a huge booty and killing hundreds of men. Byzantium surrendered, losing its independent city status.

Once he had consolidated his power, Septimius Severus launched a new campaign against the Parthians in 197 AD. His troops, embarked on warships of the *Classis Syriaca, Mesopotamica* and comprised of Praetorian *Classes*, travelled on the Euphrates, along the Roman–Parthian borders, reaching and sacking the Parthian capital, Ctesiphon. At the time of Septimius Severus, ten fleets formed part of the standing army of the Empire.

EMPLOYMENT OF THE FLEET IN CONQUEST WARS

The Conquest of Dacia (101–106 AD)
The naval aspect of the Trajanic wars against the Dacians along the river Danube mainly involved the *Classis Moesica*, although reinforced with ships of the two main *Classes Praetoriae*. The *Classis Moesica* was the real stalwart of the naval campaigns, supplementing bridges by transporting troops and supplies. Its other main duty was to penetrate as far as it could inside the enemy's territories and intercept or gather information on the Dacians. Trajan also tasked his fleet with securing and maintaining an essential link to

69 AD, A BATTLE BETWEEN THE BRITISH FLEET AND THE XIV LEGIO AND THE BATAVIANS AND THEIR CANNINEFATAE ALLIES

The scene shows a Roman warship being attacked by two enemy ships and their crews fighting on the deck; the *liburna* of the *Classis Britannica* is copied from a British Museum relief, while the captured *liburnians* of the *Classis Germanica*, manoeuvred by the men of Civilis, are copied from the fresco of Aula Isiaca. The long box projection running from bow to just short of the steering oars does not only accommodate the oarsmen, but acts as a platform from which the marines could more easily leap aboard an enemy vessel when alongside. On the prow of the British *liburna*, below a foremast with foresail set, are two parallel wales terminating forward in the *proembolion*, here not visible. Although mainly oar-powered, the *liburnae* were also fitted with a square main sail and a smaller foresail. Note the strong latticework screen to protect the rowers.

the sources of supply for the expeditionary forces. These functions were decisive for the victorious outcome of the wars.

The exploits of the *Classis Moesica* in the Trajanic wars for the conquest of the Dacia are well illustrated on Trajan's Column in Rome. The depictions are also a very good general impression of the navy's role in any larger campaigns. Along the south bank of the Danube, cargo ships (*onerariae*) were loaded with barrels, tent packs and other supplies destined for the Dacian campaign. Supplies were moved by boat along the Danube, while other boats formed a pontoon bridge for the passage of troops. The fact that after the campaign, among the *dona militaria* (military decorations) were four *Coronae Navales* (the golden crowns decorated with the prow of a ship), shows the vital role of the Imperial fleets during the campaign.

As preparation for the campaign, a canal was built in 100 AD on the Roman (south) side of the Danube, near the Iron Gates Gorge and the rapids. The canal was fitted with locks guarded by garrisons. It enabled the ships in Pannonia and Moesia to link up and operate together and to allow the whole length of the river to be navigated.

The Roman fleet in the *Bellum Germanicum et Sarmaticum* (168–180 AD)

In the wars of Marcus Aurelius, the Danubian fleets were constantly in action. They supplied and provided transport to the troops along the river and its tributaries. It was instrumental in allowing the army to pursue the Barbarians into what today are the plains of Bohemia and Hungary. In 170–171 AD the ex-Consul Marcus Valerius Maximianus was sent with *vexillationes* from *Praetoriae* and *Britannica Classes* to bring supplies for Marcus' army down to the Danube. *Mauri* Cavalrymen escorted his boats, following them along the banks of the river. So in this campaign, as well as the resident fleets (*Classis Moesica* and *Pannonica*), all the available fleets from territories not under threat were used (such as the *Classis Britannica*) and their officers were charged with the command of all the floating boats and supply ships, even bringing with them boats of their own. The *Classes Praetoriae* acted as reserve fleets with highly trained personnel.

The naval *blitzkrieg* of Septimius Severus (197 AD)

The borders with Parthia were not pacified permanently, and in 197 AD new pressures on the frontiers forced Emperor Septimius Severus to continue his march towards Syria. During the campaign, the Roman troops embarked along the Euphrates, which already at that time marked the borders between the Empire and Parthia for about 200 miles. At the point where the two rivers are closest, the Romans moved on the Tigris and captured the capital of the Parthia, Ctesiphon, by surprise. The episode is described in detail, in a picturesque way, by Herodian:

> The army, sailing in a large number of ships, was not borne to its intended destination on Roman-held shores, but after the current had carried the fleet a great distance, the legions disembarked on Parthian beaches at a spot within a few days' march of the road leading to Ctesiphon, where the royal palace of the Parthians was located. There the king was spending his time peacefully, thinking that the battles between Severus and the Hatrenians were no concern of his. But the troops of the emperor, brought by the current to these shores

against their will, landed and plundered the region, driving off for food all the cattle they found and burning all the villages as they passed. After proceeding a short distance, they stood at the gates of Ctesiphon, the capital city of the great king Artabanus. The Romans fell upon the unsuspecting barbarians, killing all who opposed them. Taking captive the women and children, they looted the entire city. After the king fled with a few horsemen, the Romans plundered the treasuries, seized the ornaments and jewels, and marched off.

Flagship, first Dacian campaign, 101–102 AD. (Casts 85–86 of scene LXXXIV–XXXV of Trajan's Column, Rome, Museo della Civiltà Romana, author's photographs, courtesy of the museum)

THE ORGANIZATION OF THE IMPERIAL ROMAN NAVY

The basic structure of the navy consisted of two *classes*, or fleets, each complemented by regional groupings of support in strategic sites. These two *classes*, based on the newly created military harbours of *Misenus* and *Classis*, enjoyed a rank comparable to that of the Pretorian Guard. According to Tacitus (Annals, 4. 5, 1): 'Italy on both seas was guarded by fleets, at Misenum and at Ravenna, and the contiguous coast of Gaul by ships of war captured in the victory of Actium, and sent by Augustus powerfully manned to the town of Forojulium' (modern Frejus). But very soon the two Italian fleets superceded the fleet at Forum Julii, which was gradually run down, until it became a simple outpost of the Misene fleet, operating until the time of Nero.

There were allied fleets in the provinces from the beginning of the Empire. They were not trusted as well as the main fleets to perform special duties, but were used in combination with the main fleets or in support of the land army. The allied fleets were soon transformed into naval branches of the Roman military structure. We should therefore not think of the Roman navy in the modern meaning of the word – i.e. an entity distinguishable from the land army – but more like a waterborne division of the army.

The hierarchy was well established: the three main fleets, as well as the provincial navies, were commanded by *praefecti* (prefects), of equestrian rank, directly under the command of the emperor and not of the Senate. They were appointed from high ranks in the army, sometimes the *praefectus* being formerly a tribune of a legion or a senior centurion. Under Claudius and Nero freedmen also began to be appointed to the command of the fleets (*CIL* VIII, 21025, career of a freedman appointed *trierarchus* of the *Classis Augusta Alexandrina*). Each commander of a provincial fleet was

Details of the flagship from the first Dacian campaign. The stempost (*prora*) of the flagship.

The stern (*puppis*) of the flagship. The flagship has two oarsmen, one of them the Emperor Trajan, who was managing the ship for public display. (Roma, Museo della Civiltà Romana, author's photograph, courtesy of the museum)

assisted by a *subpraefectus* (sometimes called *praepositus* in the *Classis Alexandrina* operating in Mauretania) and was assisted, in his administrative duties, by his *officium* composed of *librarii* and *beneficiarii*.

Admirals and commanders of squadrons were called *navarchai*, while captains were called *trierarchs*, according to Greek terminology. The senior in rank was the *navarchus princeps* or *archigubernes*, who was the main advisor of the *praefectus* (something like the *centurio primus pilus* for the *legatus legionis*). The staff of the senior and junior officers was composed of a centurion, an *optio* (deputy of the centurion) and a *suboptio*, an *armorum custos* (officer charged of the keeping of the weapons) and the *bucinator* (trumpeter). *Beneficiarius* (chief administrative officer), *secutor* (junior administrative officer), *scriba* and *librarius* (naval functionaries) composed the staff of the *trierarcha*. Ten was the usual number of ships for each naval squadron.

On the warships the marines (*milites classiarii*) formed a *centuria* under the command of the *centurion*. The naval centuria was, however, composed not only of the fighters (*propugnatores*), but also of the crews of the war machines (*balistarii*), the archers (*sagittarii*) and even the steerman, the clerks, and the oarsmen fought. The oarsmen (*remiges*) were usually handpicked men and formed part of the crew: slave labour was generally never used on the oars of a Roman galley, although occasionally some criminals or slaves were condemned to perform the duty of oarsmen on the warships.

As in the late consular age, the ship was managed by the *gubernator* or *navita* (Ovid, *Tristia*, IV, 11) – a steerman and supervisor of the operations of oaring – assisted by a *proreta*. The duty of the *proreta* was very important: stationed in the forward part of the ship, he gave information to the *gubernator* about rocks or obstacles in the ship's path. The *celeusta* or *pausarius* was the chief rowing officer. He had to ensure the rhythmical and efficient work of the rowers, as described by Seneca (*Epistulae*, 56): 'But by now I have so steeled myself against all these things that I can even put up with a coxswain's [*pausarius*'] strident tones as he gives his oarsmen the rhythm.' Sometimes a flute-player (*symphoniacus*) and a *pitulus* armed with a mallet set the pace for the oarsmen. The crew was completed by the doctor (*medicus*), the master carpenters (*fabri navales*), the quartermaster (*nauphylax*) and the *coronarius* and *victimarius* (respectively charged to garland the ship during the festivals and to offer sacrifices on behalf of the crew).

B THE FLEET OF THE EMPEROR TRAJAN AT THE CONQUEST OF DACIA, ISTRUM, 101 AD

The scene shows the river *biremes* and *triremes* of the *Classis Pannonica* on the Danube. Both ships are copied from Trajan's Column. *Liburnicae biremes* are the most common type of warship on the column, which depicts the transport of the army along the Danube. Some of them are aphract (not closed on the sides) galleys without an outrigger: the upper banks of oars are worked through a latticework screen. In other ships the oars protruded through slits below the latticeworks screen, which seems to have been conceived as a ventilation course. Also the flagship is represented with an elaborately decorated bow, stern shelter, and two helmsmen.

Stempost of a Roman *liburna*, from Trajan's Column, scene LXXXII. (Cast of the Museo della Civiltà Romana, author's photo, courtesy of the museum)

The Roman fleets of *Classis Ravenna* and *Misenum*

The creation of a new fleet at Ravenna was marked by the opening of a new canal to the river Po. Engineering works included the construction of moles, a lighthouse (*pharos*) and fortifications. Inscriptions show that the Ravenna fleet was composed mainly of light *liburnians*, *triremes*, *quadriremes* and few 'Fives'. The inscriptions show the ships of the Misenum fleet were mainly light *liburnians*, *triremes*, *quadriremes* and few 'Fives' and 'Sixes'. In the *Misenensis* fleet alone, the sources records the name of the flagship 'Six' (*hexeres*) called *Ops*.

The men of the two fleets had permanent camps in Rome, where detachments of these fleets helped to stage mock naval battles in specially constructed arenas (in which condemned criminals fought); and the marines of the *Misenensis* fleet, from the beginning of the Flavian Age (70 AD), worked the canvas awnings that protected spectators in the Coliseum[2] from the sun. During the ferocious wars of 68–69 AD, the men of these fleets were raised by Nero, Vitellius and Vespasianus to create new legions (*I* and *II Adiutrix*: Tacitus, *Histories*, I, 6; Suetonius, Galba, XII, 2[3]).

The naval bases of the *Classis Ravennatis* were at Salona, capital of Dalmatia, and Aquileia. Detachments of the *Misenensis* served at ports such as Puteoli, Centumcellae, Ostia and the new harbour of Portus built under Claudius. Misenum and Puteoli were also the main harbours for the despatches brought by Imperial couriers to and from all corners of the Empire.

These fleets were maintained in the Mediterranean (usually in small flotillas) as a political precaution against outbreaks of piracy or other local emergencies; there were no serious maritime rivals to the Roman Empire, at least until the third century AD. The main naval actions that were fought in the Mediterranean were during the civil wars. In common with the legions, fleets were commissioned to perform special duties, such as escorting important personalities. In 65 AD, the fleets were commissioned by Nero to find the treasure of Dido, Queen of Carthage, lost a thousand years before (Tacitus, *Annales*, 16, 2). Ostia was the harbour of Rome, so it was logical that from there senators and eminent personalities, under the escort of the warships of the *Classes Praetoriae*, sailed for their destinations into the provinces, or for their provincial appointments and commands. In 69 AD, by order of Galba, two *triremes* of

The stern (*puppis*) of the same *liburna*. (Rome, Museo della Civiltà Romana, author's photograph, courtesy of the museum)

2 See MAA 451: *Imperial Roman Naval Forces 31 BC–AD 500*
3 See MAA 451: *Imperial Roman Naval Forces 31 BC–AD 500*

the fleet are recorded as having escorted the new Prefect of Cylicia and Pamphylia (Tacitus, *Histories*, II, 9).

The two main fleets very quickly acquired similar duties, and changed in their composition. Some of the two fleets' bases functioned as store depots and refitting yards.

The Provincial Fleets

Regular detachments of the two main fleets were also located in the Provinces and at various strategic ports: in the east at Cyzicus, Ephesus, Pyreus (Athens); at Spalato (Split) in Illyria and at Brundysium in Italy (Brindisi); at Caralis (Cagliari) in Sardinia, at Aleria in Corsica. Panormus (Palermo) and Sciscia (Sisak) were occasional bases. Alexandria, in Egypt, which since 28 BC has been promoted to the status of a military harbour, was also a permanent base of the Misenum fleet. In time, the detachments melded with the *auxilia* fleets, forming the bulk of the local *classis* in the different regions. Very soon the vastness of the Empire compelled the Romans to create provincial fleets from these nucleii. Originally the provincial fleets were of foreign origin, and so in comparison with the *Classes Praetoriae* they were like the *auxilia* compared to the *legiones*. For this reason, in the earlier times of the Principate, service on these fleets was considered an 'inferior service', reserved for provincials.

The Rhine and Danube Fleets

In the earlier years of the Principate, during the expansion wars of the Julio-Claudian dynasty, the main function of the Roman fleets was to serve the Roman army on the Rhine and Danube. Permanent bases for detachments of the two Pretorian fleets were Bonna (Bonn), Vetera-Nigrum Pullum, Neuss, Arientsburg, Velsen and Vechten. One of the first provincial fleets to be created, under Augustus, was a fleet on the Rhine, later called *Classis Germanica*, which in 69 AD consisted of 24 ships. Doubtless, the first establishment of a naval unit on the river Rhine was during the military campaigns of Drusus the Elder, appointed by Augustus, commander in chief of the Roman army in Germania in 12 BC (Florus, Ep., II, 30, 26: 'Along the banks of the Rhine he disposed more than five hundred forts. He built bridges at Borma [*sic* – Bonna] and Gesoriacum, and left fleets to protect them').

Drusus the Elder's aim in annexing territories up to the river Elba, so as to join the Roman forces operating in Germania with those who were completing the conquest of Pannonia, could not have been achieved without a naval force able to support the land army and to exploit the numerous tributaries of the Rhine as main channels to penetrate into the Germanic interior. This was so important that it required the creation of an artificial channel, the *Fossa Drusiana*

Liburnians and *triremes* of the *Classis Ravennatis*, second Dacian campaign, 106 AD. Three longships are shown, two *liburnians* and one *triremis*, setting out from Ancona Harbour. The oar system of all three ships is shown on the outer side of the hull. The *liburnicae* show seven oars a side disposed on two levels, the other is a 'Three' with the uppermost banks rowed through a screen. (Casts 208–213 of scenes LXXIX and LXXX, Trajan's Column, Rome, Museo della Civiltà Romana, photograph courtesy of Domenico Carro)

Loading and unloading of small transport vessels on the Danube, first Dacian campaign, 101–102 AD. (Casts 80 and 87 of scene XXXIII, XXXV on Trajan's Column, Rome, Museo della Civiltà Romana, author's photograph, courtesy of the museum)

(Suetonius. *Claud*. I; Tacitus, *Annales* II 8, 1), to connect the river with the North Sea, through what the Romans called *lacus Flevus*, today's IJsselmeer. For over 20 years the main tasks of this fleet were to convey military shipments along the lower reaches of the Rhine to the sea and to contribute to the slow but determined advance eastward, along the course of the Lippe and the Main.

After the defeat of Teutoburgus, in 9 AD, and the victorious campaigns of Germanicus in 15–16 AD, the future *Classis Germanica* was reorganized. Under Tiberius, Roman policy in the area was transformed from offensive to defensive, with the consequent stabilization of the military deployment along the river, in order to safeguard and preserve the borders. In all likelihood, it was this period that saw the organization and the birth of the *Classis Germanica* in its permanent form, when it assumed the duties that it kept for the rest of its life: patrolling the middle and lower reaches of the Rhine to its mouth, controlling the Germanic tribes on its banks, and supporting and transporting troops along the river. In Germany, and as happened later in Mauretania, Britannia and Siria, the provincial fleet was born from naval units left at the end of a campaign, which were converted into a permanent local naval force, for control purposes and containment. Among the commanders of the *Classis Germanica*, in 165 AD, was a future emperor, Publius Helvius Pertinax.

The upper Danube was under the control of the *Classis Flavia Moesiaca*, which military diplomas and inscriptions of various *Classiarii* prove was established between 73 and 92 AD, but it was developed earlier, along with the first nucleus of the *Classis Flavia Pannonica*, probably at the same time

C

COMBAT BETWEEN THE MEN OF CLASSIS PANNONICA AND THE IAZYGES ON THE IRON GATES, MARCOMANNIC WARS, WINTER 173–174 AD

In the winter of 173–174 AD the *Classis Pannonica* was disabled by the freezing of the Danube and a battle took place on the ice to defeat the raiding Barbarians. In the foreground, the scene shows Roman soldiers and officers pushing back a group of Quadi and Jazigi from their ships and their buildings to the frozen water. The Roman ship on the left is a light *celox*, copied from the Alba Fucens relief. As its name implies (*celox* means 'fast', or in Greek 'racehorse', κέλητες), this kind of ship was renowned for its speed. It was smaller than the *lembos* and had a straight prow. It was useful for carrying passengers and bringing despatches, with a rowing crew of 20 or fewer oarsmen, it was perfect for operations in the Marcomannic Wars.

as the *Classis Germanica* was established. According to Starr, the creation of the *Classis Pannonica* was contemporary with, or followed, the Roman expansion in the middle and high Danube. This would date it to the Empire of Augustus, when Tiberius was establishing military operations in Pannonia in the early years of the first century AD.

Here the advance of the army was also necessarily supported by the naval contingents on the river. Perhaps at the beginning it was composed only of provincial units, and the archaeological or epigraphic evidence to date does not prove the presence of a Roman fleet at that time. Under Vespasian the trend radically changes: in fact, it is to him or to Domitian that the oldest reorganization of the area as a *limes* is attributed. Therefore, it is more plausible that Vespasian, rather than one of his sons, should be recognized as the creator of the true *Classis Pannonica* that guarded the middle reaches of the river, and as the originator of the Classis *Flavia Moesica* for the next leg, to the mouth. The epithet '*Flavia*' for both fleets attests also to this origin, unique among all the naval forces of the empire. The main port and home of the command of the fleet was Taurunum, at the confluence of the Sava and the Danube; the existence of other permanent stations is likely; the archaeological evidence (epigraphic finds and brick stamps) point to Carnuntum and Brigetium.

The basic tasks of these provincial fleets were to control the traffic and travel along and across the river, as well as establishing the first line of defence and warning of threatening behaviour from the Transdanubian populations. Again, it is very likely that both fleets played an important role in the Roman military operations on the Danube, from Trajan's Dacian wars to the wars of Marcus Aurelius against the Quadi and Marcomanni, charged with logistical tasks and troop transport along the front.

The *Classis Britannica*

The *Classis Britannica* was put together for the invasion of Britain in 43 AD, by adding several new ships to the old patrolling fleet already established in the area by Julius Caesar and by using the northern nucleus created by Caligula. In 40 AD this latter had made preparations for the invasion of Britain, choosing Boulogne as an invasion port (then known as Gesoriacum) and, according to Suetonius (Gajus, 46–47) and Dio Cassius (LIX, 25, 2) he had *triremes*, one of them even as his flagship. The bulk of these ships was stationed in the English Channel and formed the core of Claudius' invasion fleet. The *Classis Britannica* was the main fleet in the North Sea. Its main harbours were at Rutupiae (Richborough) and Dubrae (Dover), both in Kent, where archaeologists have discovered the remains of an early second-century fort and two lighthouses. The official residence of the *Praefectus* was on the cliffs at Folkstone, where a magnificent villa was built. The main duty of this fleet was to protect communications between Gaul and Britain, as well as support the armies operating in the area, as it did for the campaigns of Agricola in Caledonia. It also performed a subsidiary role in the production of iron in the mines of Kent.

Tomb relief of a *liburna* of the *Classis Britannica*, c. 100 AD. (British Museum, London, photograph courtesy of Domenico Carro)

The *Classis Syriaca*

The *Classis Syriaca* patrolled the eastern Mediterranean: Cyprus, southern Asia Minor, the eastern Aegean and Syria. According to Starr the fleet was established in the first century AD, created by Vespasian during the first Jewish–Roman war (66–73 AD); according to other scholars it was formed in support of the Parthic campaign of the Emperor Trajan. Putting aside the date of its foundation, there is evidence of Praetorian fleets in the port of Seleucia, the main base of the *Classis Syriaca*. Inscriptions from the second century prove that, despite the creation of a strong autonomous and independent provincial force, the port continued to welcome *vexillationes* of the Italian fleets, a result of the military intervention of Vespasian during the second half of the first century, which also played a role in the Trajanic Wars. In 152 AD, against a new Parthian menace, the duty of the *Classis Syriaca* was mainly to patrol the area between Alexandria and Seleucia, the Cylician coast and the port of Antioch. It was also reinforced with 200 ships from the *Classes Praetoriae*. The *Classis Mesopotamica* often worked alongside its sister fleet, in order to keep control of the regions of the newly constituted province of Mesopotamia.

Detail of a first-century fresco in the House of Atrio Corinzio. Several oared ships, possibly 'Fives', are shown in a naval battle. The blind course as a permanent louvre/sidescreen that both the ships show makes it more certain that they are *cataphractae* 'Fives' of old Romano-Carthaginian design, a design still used for big ships in the first century AD. (In situ, Herculaneum, sector B74)

In Egypt, in the Empire of Augustus, a detachment of the *Misenensis* became the new *Classis Augusta Alexandrina* and another fleet was created at Arsinoe, on the Red Sea (*Classis Arabica*). The main duty of the former was an unusual one, but of vital importance: to safeguard the grain supplies from Egypt destined for the capital, Rome.

Detachments from the fleets of both *Syriaca* and *Alexandrina* also supervised the western area of the Mediterranean, from their bases in Caesarea, in Mauretania. The origins of the establishment of a fleet in the western African corner of the Roman Empire are linked to the definitive conquest of the area, which began in 40 AD under Caligula and was finally completed when Claudius pacified the new province. In the usual normalization process, the Romans decided to give a permanent shape to the naval deployment that had supported, supplied and assisted the conquest expedition. The structure of the Roman naval presence in Mauretania was unusual among the provincial fleets, as it consisted of a 'permanent detachment' of elements of the *Classis Alexandrina* (although in other parts, detachments of Pretorian fleets were the bulk of the naval defence of the territory). Regarding the presence of a detachment (*vexillatio*) of the *Classis Syriaca* in the area (*CIL* VIII, 9358, 9363, 9385), Reddè and Könen have recently supported the theory that ships from the Syrian fleet were sent to *Mauretania Caesarensis* in the second half of the second century AD, to increase the naval contingent in the province, which was quantitatively insufficient to transport soldiers, during the war against the Moors undertaken by Antoninus Pius and then restarted during the reign of Marcus Aurelius.

From 180 or 188 AD, however, the area was under the surveillance of a newly constituted fleet, the *Classis Nova Libica* (inscription from Cyrta, *CIL* VIII, 7030), perhaps to be identified, according to Pavis d'Escurac, with the *Classis Africana Commodiana*. It may have been established after 170 AD to patrol the waters of Western Africa and prevent external attacks, following the wars of Marcus Aurelius. Given the size of the port, not many ships could

Scene of *Naumachia* in a fresco from the Macellum's courtyard. Both ships are shown from their prows. Despite the damage to the fresco, the rams, the apotropaic eyes and the marines forming their crews are still visible. (Pompeii first century AD, in situ, photograph courtesy of Domenico Carro)

have been left in this province, and these would have been largely *liburnians*. Their tasks were the control of the coasts, the fight against piracy and the protection of merchant ships arriving and departing from Mauretania, and of course, troop transport to and from the province.

The frontier in Anatolia between the Black Sea and the Syrian Plain was one of the most important Roman borders. Roman fleets were set up on the coasts of the Anatolian Black Sea. Trapezus (nowadays Trabzon) was the major base of the Roman fleet in the area, the *Classis Pontica*, created under Nero, the harbour of which was reconstructed by Hadrian (Arrian, *Circum*., 16; Cassio Dio, 69, 5, 3). The fleet was responsible for the eastern and southern sectors of the Black Sea, and in 152 AD, due to the pressure of the Parthians on the Euphrates borders, moved its main base westward, at Cyzicus, in Propontis. Here it stayed permanently during the Marcomannic Wars, although always patrolling the northern coasts of Asia Minor and having detachments in Trapezus.

The ships of these fleets were mainly light galleys (*liburnicae*) as it is expressly stated by Tacitus (Hist., III, 47) for the *Classis Pontica* and the *Classis Britannica*. According to Agricola, 28: '… a Usipian cohort, which had been levied in Germany and transported into Britain … having killed a centurion and some soldiers, who, to impart military discipline, had been incorporated with their ranks … embarked on board three swift galleys (*liburnicae*) with pilots (*gubernatores*) pressed into their service …'.

IMPERIAL ROMAN WARSHIPS AND BOATS

The evidence of Tacitus, in his works (*Annales*, *Historia*, *Agricola* and *Germania*), is fundamental in an attempt to determine the types of warships in use in the Imperial fleet during the early Empire. Tacitus mentions no type of warship higher than 'Fours'. Moreover, this mention of the *quadriremes* is linked to the episode of the Naumachia in the Fucine lake (*Annales*, 12. 56, 2: 'Claudius equipped galleys with three (*triremes*) and four (*quadriremes*) banks of oars, and nineteen thousand men'; and Suetonius, Claud., XII, 6:

TRIREMIS AND LIBURNICA BIREMIS, FIRST AND SECOND CENTURY AD

1: The *cataphracta triremis* is copied from the Pozzuoli relief (see page 8). Its sidescreen shows the emergence of the oars, shields the (necessary) ventilation course and oar ports, and is fitted to a *parodos* on which decksoldiers could stand and fight. On the relief from which the ship is copied, the main deck soldiers rather than oarsmen are visible. Facing them, and shown bigger (and hence more important), stands a man (*keleustis trierarches*), behind whose head the tiller is held by the helmsman sitting high in the stern.

2: The *liburnica biremis* is copied from Trajan's Column. The ordinary complement of a *liburna* was of 30 to 40 men, according to Tacitus (*Hist*., X, 1, 3). A fully sized *liburna* (*biremes*) had an oarcrew of 50 men, but the information from Tacitus proves that there were also smaller craft with a liburnian oar system and two levels of single manned oars. The smaller liburnians had two banks of oars with one man per oar, making the ship similar to a *biremis*. However, their size could vary. According to Propertius (*Elegies*, III, 11), the *liburnae* were *rostratae*. This is widely confirmed by the iconography, which shows their sharply pointed beaks.

Fresco from the Suburbans *Termae*, *Natatio* of the *Frigidarium*, Pompeii, 54–68 AD. An oared Roman warship under way seen from the port side. There are two big apotropaic eyes on the well preserved stempost. Note the long box-like projection running from the bow to just short of the steering oars, although in this model there is not room for oarsmen. This is a system used on many ships, from *triremes* on, to afford better protection to the men and oars against any attempt by an enemy vessel to come alongside and break off the blades. It also sheltered the rowers from missiles. Louvres were added to provide ventilation. (In situ, Pompeii, photograph courtesy of Domenico Carro)

'Even when he was on the point of letting out the water from Lake Fucinus he gave a sham sea-fight first … At this performance a Sicilian and a Rhodian fleet engaged, each numbering twelve triremes, and the signal was sounded on a horn by a silver Triton, which was raised from the middle of the lake by a mechanical device'. The ships in these passages are mentioned as *tectae* (i.e. *cataphractae*) – in other words, closed ships.

According to Morrison, this is due to the circumstance that after the age of the great galley battles for control of the Mediterranean Sea, the age that ended with the battle of Actium, the great ships were no longer necessary and largely disappeared, especially the monster *Polyremes*.

This is not completely true. Ships were always distinguished as *naves maioris formae* (the larger type, comprising 'Fives' and above) or *naves minoris formae* (the smaller type, 'Fours' and below). Of course, big ships were still in use in the fleet of *Forum Julii* (Frejus), garrisoned by the galleys taken from Cleopatra and Antony. This fleet included rammed ships (*naves rostratae*) of the category of 'Threes', 'Fives' and more, as it is possible to understand from the different sizes of the sockets of the rams in the Nikopolis monument: 'Sixes' (*exereis*), 'Sevens', (*eptereis*), 'Eights' (*oktereis*), 'Nines' (*ennereis*) and 'Tens' (*dekereis*). They were manned by strong oar crews (*valido remige*). Moreover, the list of the sources (CIL, AE, CPL, Ephem. Epigr. and the Greek inscriptions of Syria) show – although in small numbers – 'Fives' and 'Sixes' were included in the two main Imperial fleets. In the first century AD a 'Six' (the *Ops*) is remembered as the flagship of the senior fleet at Misenum. But we also have mention, in a later age, of a *quinquiremes* named *Augustus*, on which a certain *classiarius* of the Ravenna fleet (Titus Fulvius Nepos) served for 24 years in the second and the third century AD. It is important also to understand the life of an ancient ship, if Nepos' 24 years of military service were all performed on this ship, which is not clear from his stele.

It is certainly true that the presence of smaller ships in the fleets shows a change of Roman naval strategy: naval resources were concentrated on duties which required speed and agility rather than maximum fighting power, such as the prevention of piracy or more formal duties, such as providing official transport for members of Imperial families or other high dignitaries. However, the fact that a small number of *polyremes* was still present in the fleets suggests that the possibility of major sea clashes was still taken into consideration. Instead, *triremes* were posted at strategic points in the provinces to provide a Roman naval presence. These were probably also built by the allied cities, because Tacitus refers to them as *sociae triremes*.

Light ships were employed also in the *Naumachiae* (Augustus, 2 BC), but, according to the *Res Gestae Divi Augusti* (23) they were *rostratae naves*, that is *triremes* and *biremes* (or maybe *liburnians*) and many smaller ships (*naves minores*): 'I gave the people the spectacle of a naval battle beyond the Tiber … In this spectacle thirty beaked ships, triremes or biremes, and a large number of smaller vessels met in conflict. In these fleets there fought about three thousand men exclusive of the rowers.' A list, given by Aulus Gellius in his *Noctes Atticae* (X, 25, 5) describes a great variety of vessels, ranging from the bigger boats to the simplest small ones:

The names of ships which I recalled at the time are these: merchant-ships [*gauli*], cargo-carriers [*corbitae*], skiffs [*caudicae*], warships [*longae*], cavalry-transports [*hippagines*], cutters [*cercuri*], fast cruisers [*celoces*], or, as the Greeks call them, κέλητες, barques [*lembi*], smacks [*oriae*], sailing-skiffs [*lenunculi*], light galleys [*actuariae*], which the Greeks call ἱστιοκόποι or ἐπακτρίδες, scouting-boats [*prosumiae* or *geseoretae* or *oriolae* or *stlattae*], galliots [*scaphae*], tenders [*pontones*], flat-boats [*vectoriae*], vetutiae moediae [*mydia*], yachts [*phaseli*], pinnaces [*parones*], long-galliots [*myioparones*], scullers' boats [*lintres*], caupuls [*caupuli*], arks [*camarae*], fair-weather craft [*placidae*], pinks [*cydarum*], lighters [*rotariae*], spy-boats [*scaphae*].

Relief from Marcus Aurelius' Column, showing the transport on carriages of pontoon bridges and boats. (Rome, in situ, photograph courtesy of Domenico Carro)

Boats

Simple boats were not less important for Roman warfare than warships, and Civilis in his parade on the Rhine with the captured Roman fleet showed beside them war-boats having each a crew of 30 or 40 men. Sometimes the boats were fitted with particoloured plaids for sails, which made a fine show and helped their movement. The finds and excavation of two river boats (referred to by archaeologists as ships E and G) in the San Rossore area give us a good idea of dimensions of these *scaphae*: one of the boats, dated to the early second century, is 8.20m long, and 1m wide. The other is 8m long and of similar width. The small structure of the boats, employed for navigation along the river Arno, with flat keels, straight sides and raised ends, immediately reminds one of the boats visible on the reliefs of Trajan's Column, dedicated to the transport on the Danube of the legionary supplies. The dating of both boats to the early second century has been possible thanks to some weights and coins from the time of Hadrian. A third boat (ship H) from the site of the same typology but smaller has been found covering the other two.

The military use of boats to build a pontoon bridge for the passage of the soldiers is a practice well documented on the Trajan and Marcus Aurelius columns. Pontoons are shown being transported on wagons, probably of the type known as *ratis* or *ratiariae*, a kind of boat made by the military for wars of conquest. These pontoons were built across the river and then dismantled after use. The technique of building and defend these pontoons is well described by Cassius Dio (LXXI, 2, fragments from Suidas):

Rivers are bridged by the Romans with the greatest ease, since the soldiers are always practising bridge-building, which is carried on like any other warlike exercise, on the Ister [Danube], the Rhine, and the Euphrates. Now the method of procedure … is as follows. The ships by means of which the river is to be bridged are flat-bottomed [as in the Pisa specimens], and these are anchored a little way up-stream from the spot where the bridge is to be

Relief from Marcus Aurelius' Column, showing a pontoon bridge on the Danube. (Rome, in situ, photograph courtesy of Domenico Carro)

27

Pozzuoli reliefs, detail of a *trireme* stern.

constructed. Then, when the signal is given, they first let one ship drift down-stream close to the bank that they are holding; and when it has come opposite to the spot that is to be bridged, they throw into the stream a wicker-basket filled with stones and fastened by a cable, which serves as an anchor. Made fast in this way, the ship remains in position near the bank, and by means of planks and bridge-work, which the vessel carries in large quantity, a floor is at once laid to the landing-place. Then they send down another ship at a little distance from the first, and another one beyond that, until they have extended the bridge to the opposite bank. The ship that is nearest the enemy's bank carries towers upon it and a gate and archers and catapults.

The evolution of the *biremes* (*dikrotos*)

The *biremes* are mentioned by Tacitus as being part of the Germanic fleet, together with ships having a single bank of oars. It is clear from the representations that the *biremes* used by the Imperial fleet were mainly of Liburnian type – fast and smaller warships. The seagoing *biremes* of the British and Germanic fleets were almost certainly the largest and strongest examples of these *liburnicae biremes*. The heavier of them were decked to protect the rowers, like the *cataphracta* of the British Museum's relief. The length of these ships was about 30.5m (100ft), with a beam of about 5.5m (18ft), and a displacement of 5 tons. Their complement was a force of marines and oarsmen, with numbers varying according to circumstances.

The *biremes* of the *Classis Moesiaca* or *Pannonica* are clearly depicted on Trajan's Column, where Trajan is embarked on the Danube on an Imperial galley with two levels of eight oars a side, the lower ones are rowed through oar ports and the upper ones through a latticework screen. The screen is made up of a course of units, composed of the typical X sign framed and slightly wider than high, with a slit below the lower horizontal side.

The evolution of the *triremes* (*trieres*)

The *triremes* (or 'Three') was the largest ship known in any provincial fleet, and one inscription from Boulogne (CIL XIII, 3564) confirms that the *Classis Britannica* had at least one of this kind of ship. The 'Three' was also the main flagship of many Imperial fleets, like that of Germanicus on the Rhine. The *Praetoria Triremis* was, for instance, the flagship of the Rhine fleet at the time

---

 QUINQUIREMES AND QUADRIREMES, FIRST CENTURY AD

1: The *quinquiremes* is copied from the ships fresco from Pompeii. The stempost on many ships of the period has kept the prominent outward curve of earlier times. In contrast to the *quinquiremes* of the last centuries of the Consular Age, the early Imperial 'Fives' have an oar system of quite a different design. A panel was usually built on the side of the hull in which three levels of oar ports *quincunx* fashion were located. In the original painting the panel seems to stand out more from the ship's sides than on the Consular 'Fives'.

2: The *quadriremes* is based on the fresco from the Aula Isiaca, the Herculaneum paintings and the relief of the Duke of Medina. In the Imperial age *quadriremes* had two banks of oars per side with two men on each oar, with a total minimum of 88 oarsmen on one side and 176 in total, to a maximum of 236 men. The *quadriremis* was more or less the same size as a 'Three'. The main difference was that the deck level was a little lower, considering that it had only two banks of oars. But it was speedier and with a capacity of 60 tons, it could carry 75 fighting men, apart from the oarsmen.

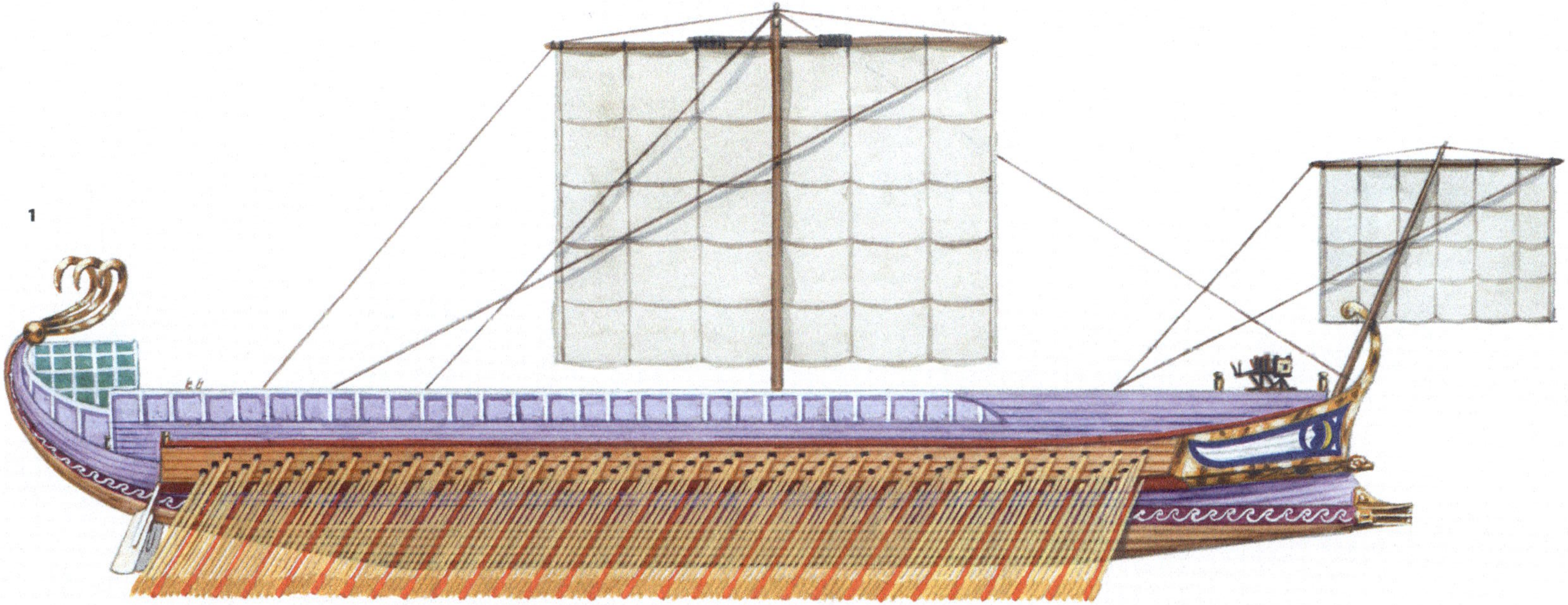

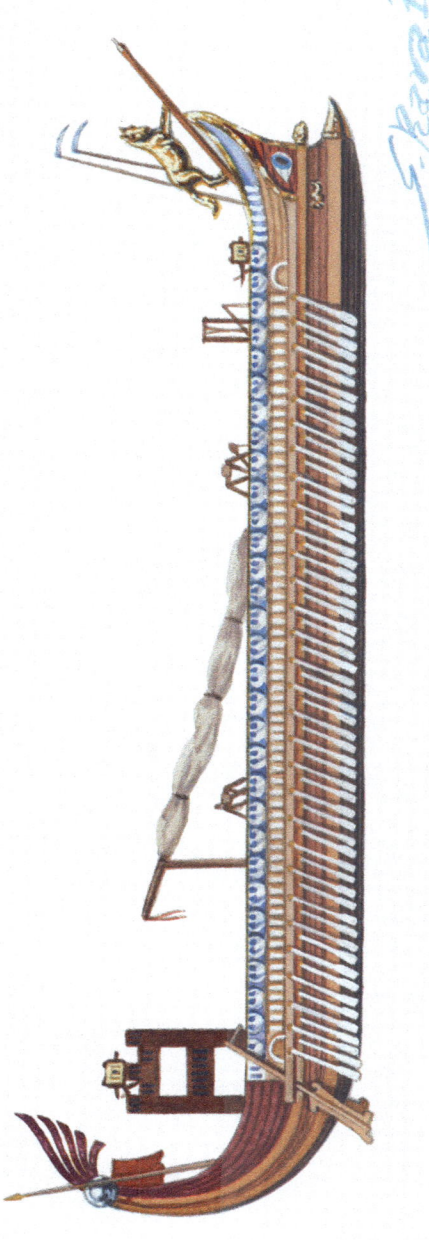

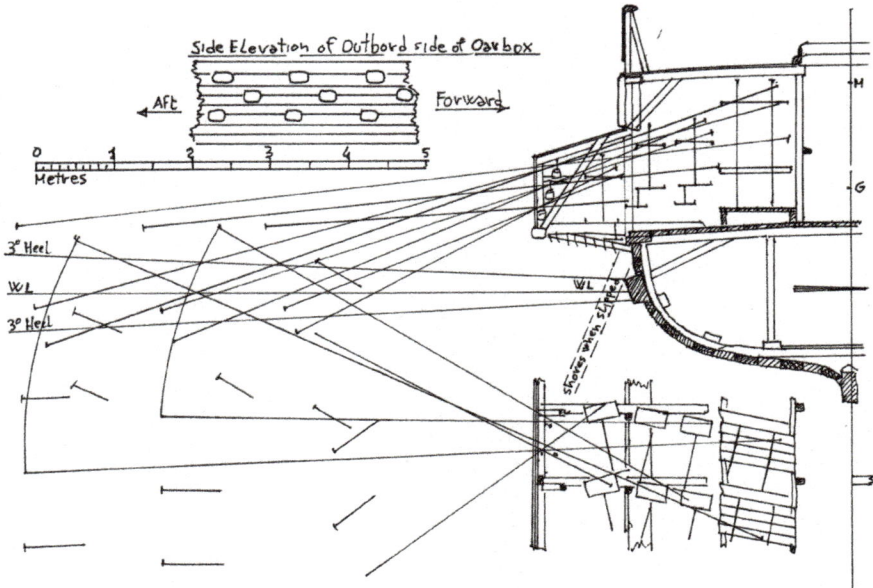

Reconstruction of the rowing system of the 'Fives' with decked hulls in the ships fresco. The top oar is shown worked by standing men. Representations show that in the typical cataphract galley of the time the upper banks of rowers were completely closed in by walls that rose to the projection of the oar boxes or, if none existed, to the gunwhale. (Drawing by Andrea Salimbeti, ex Morrison and Coates)

Boat shed frescos from Pompeii, first century AD. The fresco show two pairs of ships in their *navalia*, or port. They are shown half front, drawn up out of water in the open end of some boat sheds. The right-side ship is similar to the ship in the Isis fresco. Again, like in the Isis fresco, on the ship on the left the stempost curves aft in the Roman way, while that of the right-hand ship curves forward in the Carthaginian style. The ships are probably 'Fives' of the *Misenensis Classis*. Note the forecastle of considerable size added just behind the stempost. (Naples, National Archaeological Museum, inv. nos 8604, 8605 and 8606: B.955.956, photograph courtesy of Domenico Carro with permission of the museum)

of Cerialis in 70 AD. Tacitus, in his histories (V, 22–23) remembers when it was captured by the Germans. In AD 47 General Corbulo brought his 'Threes' through the main channels and other craft through creeks and canals.

In the first century AD, the *triremis* was characterized by its oar system, which was made of three superimposed and staggered banks of seated oarsmen, the *thalamites* at the lower level, the *zygites* above them and the *thranites* above them. However, the number of non-rowing crew would have varied in the Roman Imperial Navy. Under campaign conditions the numbers of embarked marines and sailors on each ship could have been considerable. The type of *triremes* used by the Romans at that time were either *cataphractae* (decked) either *aphractae* (open).

From Pozzuoli we have a very detailed representation of two *cataphractae triremes* of the *Misenensis* fleet. One of the ships has a large main ram and a *proembolion* – an upper ram. Behind the stempost on the foredeck there is a tower, indicating that the ship belongs to one of the larger types. There is an *epotìs* forward of a long rectangular sidescreen from under which are emerging three 'layers' of oars. The oars lie one on top of the other, and thus presumably emerge from oar ports one vertically disposed over the other, as in the late consular ship on the Ostia relief. The stern is highly decorated and the *aplustre* is very large. There is a *parasimon* at the base of the stempost.

The other ship presents all the same features (with one exception), but is smaller in size. Unlike the other, this ship has a *stylis* from which a pennant (*vexillum navale*) is flying. In the bow the second ship appears to have two *parasima*, one facing forward on the *epotìs* and one facing sideways. Her oars seem to be lighter, similarly in three layers (so it is a 'Three') but *en èchelon*, and are seen to emerge from the oarbox on the side of the ship. Both the ships have been confirmed as being from the early period of Empire. The use of the Greek type of *trireme*, characterized by the upper lever of rowers arranged in an outrigger, persisted.

Beside it, the Phoenician model, with the topmost bank of the rowers placed in ports which pierced the hull, was also employed and, by this time, gradually came to predominate. The Roman *triremis* was somewhat wider than the Greek one, with its oars placed within the span of the hull. This is, for example, visible on the ships of the Pompeii frescoes. The detail of the warships represented there gives us incredible details of the colour and shape of the *cataphractae triremis* in the Flavian Age. The large number of supports required when building such a ship, as depicted on these frescos, indicates that they are large ships, wide and prone to their sides dropping when supported only on the keel (*spina, tropis*). Only a few supports would have been needed to keep the ship upright on a slip if they were ships inferior to the 'Three' in size.

Boat shed frescos from Pompeii, first century AD. One of these *quinquiremes* has a deep oar panel, which has three rows of oar ports, *quincunx* fashion. Over the oar panel there is room for a ventilation course with the *pàrodos* on the upper surface of the outboard of a substantial bulwark. On each side of the stempost an eye decorates the side timbers of the bow, terminating in the *epotis* on the half-frontal face of which there is a *paràsimon*. This *parasimon* forms an angle with the edge of the oar panel and there is a boss or knob at the top of the angle. Two bollards are visible on each side of the upper edges of the foredeck bulwarks, one near the stempost and one further aft. The two ships appear to be built with rams above the waterline (*anasteiroi*). (Naples, National Archaeological Museum, inv. nos 8604, 8605 and 8606: B.955. 956, photograph courtesy of Domenico Carro with permission from the museum)

In Trajan's 'Three' in Ancona harbour the *thranite* oarsmen are working through the latticework units under each of which is a slit separated from the next by a short upright. It seems, therefore, that here the *thranite* oars will have emerged from the *parexeiresia* beneath the ventilation. The *zygian* oars would have emerged immediately below and above the middle wale, while the *thalamian* oars are immediately above the lowest wale. The deck is a bulwark and the shifting of the thranite oars is shown from the lattice course to the slits below it.

The evolution of the *quadriremis* and *quinquiremis*

Quadriremis with lattice work, like those of the late Republican Alba Fucentia graffito, are not particularly visible in the iconography (although some authors suggest that it can be seen in the ships of the *Atrio Corinzio* in Herculaneum). However, the employment of this kind of ship by the Praetorian fleets is widely attested in the epigraphic sources.

The representation of the 'Fives' is, on the other hand, noteworthy. A good example of early *quinquiremis* of the period is shown in the fresco of the *Aula Isiaca*, today lost, but of which some drawings still exist. Previously considered a representation of a *quadriremes* (because of a presumptive fourth row of oars appearing under an oarpanel from which three rows of oars seems to emerge), it was later correctly interpreted by Morrison and Basch as a 'Five'. The so-called 'fourth row of oars' was explained as the ship is represented beached, in comparison with Pompeian frescoes that show oared warships hauled up in ship sheds. The scene shows the mythical Trojan prince Paris helping Helen as she descends a ladder from the stern of a ship with three levels of oar ports *quincunx*-fashion in the portside with a deep projecting oarbox. This three-level ship is similar to the old Hellenistic and Roman models, for example the one represented in the Ostia relief is a 'Five'. The ship, of which a good part of the stern section is shown, resembles some ships represented on Octavian coins minted in Lugdunum and a three-level ship shown on Trajan's Column that has a course of latticework above the oar panel. The stern gives the clue to the

Fresco from the house of the priest Amandus, Pompeii, 54–68 AD. The fresco shows part of the starboard side and the bow of a *quinquiremes* that is coming into view from behind a rocky cliff. There is possibly some indication of oars on her port side. (In situ, Pompeii, photograph courtesy of Domenico Carro)

function of the latticework course as louvres, exactly as on the Octavian coins and on the Trajan's Column ships. The deck, with its bulwark, would have surmounted the latticework ventilation course.

The best representation of an Imperial *quinquiremis* is on a fresco, preserved in the house of the priest Amandus, at Pompeii. The ship, entirely white-painted, has a stempost curving aft in the Roman fashion, a high foredeck with a high bulwark and a main deck with a waist-high bulwark hung with shields, the latter crowded with armed men. Below deck a course of curved stanchions is visible, as in the most ancient Greek warships, but unlike them, this is 'blind', with no oarsmen shown in between the stanchions. Beneath the blind course, oars can be seen emerging from the ship's hull at three levels. The same characters are visible in another scene that shows the engagement of three *quinquiremes*, from the house of the Atrio Corinzio of Herculaneum (see page 23). The ships show, as in the ship of the Amandus's house, decks crowded with men armed with spears and shields, a waist-high guard-rail, the blind course below deck and the roughly painted oar system emerging below the blind course. Because the stempost curves forward in the old Carthaginian fashion and it having no shields on its guard rail, Morrison interpreted it as a historical scene of battle between Romans and Carthaginians. However, the presence of a tower on deck shows that this is a Roman model, inspired by ancient Romano-Carthaginian 'Fives'.

The evolution of the *liburna*

The *liburna* was the commonest warship of the period. Fast and small, because it was originally built for reconnaissance and for piratical activities, and adopted from the Illyrians by the Romans, it was, after the battle of Actium, the main ship of the provincial fleets. The main difference between the *liburna* and other ships, and especially from the *triremes*, *quadriremes* and *quinquiremes*, was not necessarily its system of oarage, but its construction. This is the reason why *liburnian biremes*, *triremes* and even *deceres* are mentioned in the sources.

F

LIBURNA, 200 AD

The *liburnians* were probably adopted by the Romans because they were fast, small and light vessels. They were possibly developed to suit the needs of the Imperial navy in distant provinces of the Empire as well as in the Mediterranean. Modifications such as greater protection against missiles most likely reduced the liburnians' original speed. The liburnians of Septimius Severus at the siege of Byzantium were presumably cataphract, otherwise they could scarcely have been very effective in the face of the missiles of the powerful Byzantine artillery. A reconstruction of a light 50-oared liburnian, painted according to its role of exploratory ship (*navis lusoria*), is shown here. The oars are on two levels without outriggers, which accords as closely as possible to the available evidence both literary and iconographical from the first and second centuries AD. The ship shown here, according to the Morrison reconstruction, has light protection for the oarcrew shaped like a wooden canopy supported on its outboard edges by braced pillars set in the topwale. Side protection is by screens that are let down as required. It is the same protective structure shown in some ships on Trajan's Column and in the image of the *liburna* in the British Museum. The reconstruction displaces about 15 tonnes and is 18m on the waterline. A sprint speed of just over 7 knots should be attainable from these kind of ships, according to Coates and Morrison.

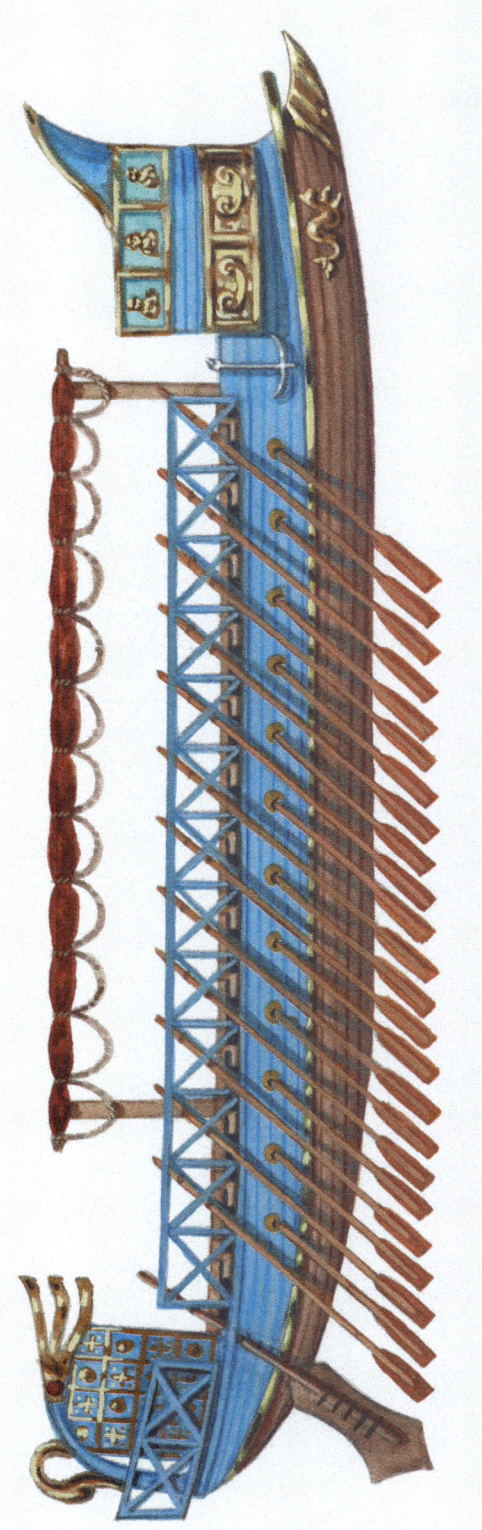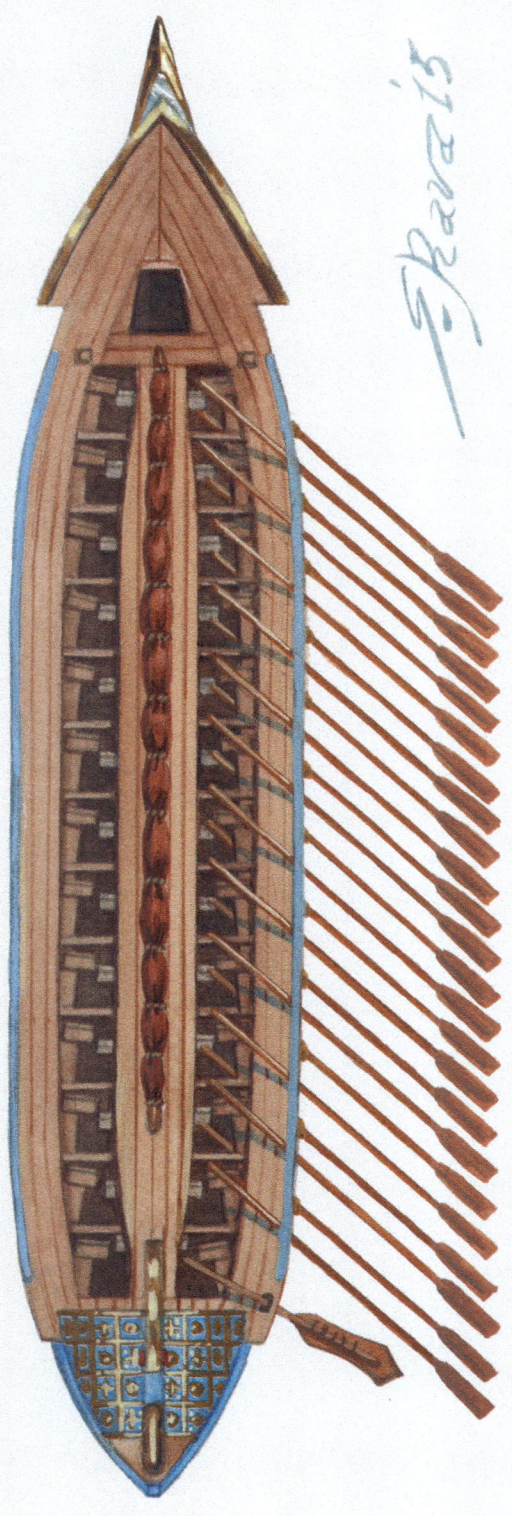

Ghyteion model, end of first century BC–first century AD. This model of a Roman warship was found in the sea off Ghyteion. It shows a warship with a ram, probably a small *liburnica*, although the kind of ship is not clearly identifiable. There are no clues to the oar system except possibly the line of holes above the lower wale. Signs of the shield-like ornaments on the side of the bulwark are visible. Although the holes are not large enough for oar ports, they may indicate where the emerging oars could be attached. However, the holes could simply be destined for the attachment of another wale. (Previously in Sparta Museum, inv. 936–943, now destined for the new museum of Laconia, author's photograph, courtesy of the museum)

The Ghyteion model is a good model of an early Imperial *liburna*, with its deck made up of a foredeck with no bulwark (and aft of it a space surrounded by a 'planked' bulwark, higher in the bow and becoming lower as it approaches the stern). The *parodos*, the gangway on both sides, is positioned outboard of the raised woodwork running along the vessel's sides, above the level of the deck (a substantial bulwark). On the port and starboard sides the deck is supported by stanchions, which continue downwards to rest on the outer wale above the waterline. By curving outwards they also serve to support the *parexeiresia* (the outriggers through which the oarsmen worked their oars), which are barely shown on the port side, with an *epotìs* (the ear-like projection on each side of the bow of a warship formed by a beam lying athwartships at the forward end of the outriggers or oarboxes).

The best representation of a second century *liburnae* is visible on Trajan's Column, on which are shown eight different types of *liburnicae biremes*. They present the following characteristics:

- a latticework ventilation course, of more or less solid structure
- a deck
- no bulwark
- the emergence of the upper oars over the topwale and below the screen

The *hexeris* or 'Six' and the *deceris*

The *hexeris* was the biggest ship mentioned in the epigraphic sources to have been in service in the regular units of the Praetorian fleet of Misenum, and is noted on a naval tombstone of the second century AD (CIL, X, 3560; CIL X, 3611). Therefore, this kind of ship was in service for at least three centuries.

Liburna, first Dacian campaign, 101–102 AD. The ship has a stern shelter (*skini*). The sails are missing and the rowing system is nine oars a side, divided in two levels. The upper level of the oars is shown through the usual latticework screen. (Casts 82–83 of scene XXXIII on Trajan's Column, Rome, Museo della Civiltà Romana, photo courtesy of Domenico Carro)

Suetonius attests that ships bigger than *triremes* were in use in the Roman Imperial fleet. According to *Life of Caligula* (37) he mentions that the emperor built *liburnian* galleys with ten banks of oars (*deceres liburnicae*), aboard which he might recline at table and coast along the shores of Campania amid songs and choruses. These ships were luxurious, like the monster-ships of the

Hellenistic Suzerains. But we know that some time after Caligula's death *liburnicae deceres* were used by Claudius for his military operations in Mauretania. These ships were not built especially by Claudius; they were Caligula's ships reused by his successor for military purposes.

The remains of two ships were salvaged from Lake Nemi in the early 1930s, but destroyed during World War II. The surviving hull of the first Nemi ship, built as a pleasure ship for the Emperor Caligula to the design of a *deceris*, measured 71.3m x 20m x 2m. The second one was 73m x 24m x 2.5m in height. Italian archaeologists have attempted the reconstruction of the starboard outrigger of one of them, which imitated that of a big warship. According to this reconstruction, the starboard outrigger pressed against cross-beams, which ended with the bronze heads of a lion and a panther. These were the bases for the steering lee board and for the entrance stairs. The rest of the outrigger was suspended from the upper cross-beams, beginning with that at the top of the stairs. The steering device had a full weight of 850kg and was leaning and lashing against the first lower cross beam and against the other two upper beams. Lashings were not very tight and the heavy device was probably suspended with a hoist; so the helmsman was standing on a catwalk after the stock of the rudder.

Liburna, second Dacian Campaign, 106 AD. The ship shows modification not seen on the other *liburnicae* ships on Trajan's Column. The ship does not have the narrow wale which housed the slits under the usual lattice units, despite the continuation of the frame sides. (Casts 216–217 of scene LXXXII, Trajan's Column, Rome, Museo della Civiltà Romana, author's photograph, courtesy of the museum)

The *actuaria* and the *oneraria*

The *actuaria* was one of the various types of smaller ships with a specialised function – an oared troop transport – and was built in large numbers for specific campaigns, such as the invasion of Britain by Claudius. It was a sort of small galley powered by 50 men (25 per side in a single bank), fitted with a projecting forefoot and with a curved prow (Lucianus, *Vera Historia*, 1, 5, calling it *Akatos*). These characteristics allowed it to be widely used in support of the military. Tacitus' description (*Annals*, II,6) of the fleet preparing to invade Batavia corresponds to this kind of ships, as well as to the transport-ships.

Many of the ships shown on Trajan's Column are simply rowed military transports. Merchant ships and ship owners were contracted – or in some circumstances compelled – to act as the logistical support to the army. These

Reconstruction of the hull of one of the Nemi ships, 39 AD. (Nemi, Museo delle Navi Romane, photograph courtesy of Domenico Carro)

LEFT
Medusa's head, bronze appliqué from the first Nemi ship, 39 AD. This head, an example of fine craftsmanship, was positioned very high on the ship, because the shape of the face takes on a vivid expression when seen from below.

RIGHT
Lion's head crowning the rudder shaft, bronze appliqué from the first ship of Nemi, 39 AD. The lion's head was a typical ornamental motif on Roman vessels, especially warships, on which the first ship of Nemi was modelled. (Rome, Museo Nazionale delle Terme, author's photos, courtesy of the museum)

onerariae had, on average, a carrying capacity of 60 to 150 tons. Some of them had a concave prow with a jutting cutwater while others had a very rounded bow. Trajan's Column, as well as that of Marcus Aurelius, show clearly the kind of *onerariae* used by the Imperial navy: some ships are destined for horse transport, others are decked cargo vessels. They had a single level of oars rowed over the top wale. A big vessel, a large merchant *oneraria*, is represented with a furled main sail.

Structure and construction

Until the first century AD, the traditional system of building a warship was to start with the construction of the ship's shell. The ships were built entirely from timber. The shipwright (*faber navalis*) shaped and fitted each plank on every side to form the hull, using some laths as templates, to define the shape of the hull. Only when the shell was ready were ribs and planks inserted to reinforce its structure from the inside, through joints made of mortises and tenons (*harmoniai*). This system is known as the carvel shipbuilding method. The shipwright arranged the planks to shape a smooth skin by setting them edge to edge (a technique of Punic origin) and locking them together with close-set mortise and tenon joints. A huge number of symmetrical mortises were cut along the edges of the jointed timbers, which were juxtaposed to allow the insertion of the wooden tenons, which would hold the planks together. The hull's timbers were placed in tiers, the spacing of which did not exceed 45cm. The frames were then joined with copper spikes, usually driven up pine dowels which had been inserted into holes drilled through the frame and plank. An

G

HEXERIS AND *ACTUARIA*, SECOND HALF OF THE SECOND CENTURY AD

1: This reconstructed *hexeris* is, based on Viereck's reconstruction, dated 117 AD. The dimensions suggested by Pitassi for such a ship are an overall length of 57m (186ft), with an overall beam of 10.4m (34ft) and a deck above the waterline of about 3.4m. According to the naval engineer Viereck and more recently Beike, it provides a clear illustration of the equipment of the bigger ships: the *hexeris* had four torsion-operated throwing machines (with cylinder compression) on the fighting high towers, and another three out of many defences on the bridge, of which the most powerful machine was in the bow.

2: The *actuaria* is reconstructed according to the mosaics of Ostia, and the structure and the colours of the *Alkedo*. Note the reconstructed colours of the warship. The white painting is correct for the *Alkedo* wreckship with red or red ochre edges applied over the white lead layer. The *quinquiremes* of the Amandus fresco is also painted white.

1

2

inner lining of planks was then laid down and fastened to the frames. Lines of thick broad planks (wales) were attached to the ship's sides: and especially in the warships of any size there was usually a wale at the waterline as protection against ramming and another at the top of the hull (gunwale).

In the warships this construction technique allowed a more robust and lightweight hull, so increasing the length of the ships, the numbers of oars and the speed of the galleys. The nails used in the construction were of various type and size: from 2cm to over 50cm, from those of a quadrangular cut with pyramid-shaped heads to those with flattened heads with small bulges, which gave them a better grip on the lead sheets lining the hull. Chemical and spectographical analysis of the nails of the Nemi ships has revealed the extremely high quality of the metals used. The low and sleek warships – with a typical ratio of length on the waterline to a structural depth of hull of between 12:1 and 14:1 – had to be built to a very high standard, which required great skill. Nails of different dimensions, in bronze and iron, of Augustan age, have been found in Pisa's canteer, where several ships and boats of various periods of Roman history have been excavated and are still under excavation.

The wood employed varied according to the availability and the place. Fir was used for *nave A* (ship A) from Pisa (2nd–3rd century AD), although the ship is a merchant vessel. The ship *Alkedo* (seagull), which was also found in Pisa, dated to about 10 AD by amphorae of Dressel 2-4 typology and therefore from the Augustan age, was built completely of oak. The shape of the ship, a small river *scapha* similar to a small *actuaria* or river *liburna*, is identical to some on Trajan's Column. When the *Alkedo* was found, a rope was still fastened to the iron ring of the dock to which she was attached. The wreck is 11.70m long and 2.80m wide. The structure was well preserved, which gave archeologists a good idea of its shape; it was fitted with six rowing benches set at regular intervals. Externally the bulwarks were reinforced with two square gunwales running parallel over the quick work. Oar ports along the bulwarks were protected with leather and fixed down with a line of bronze rivets. A small lead plate shows a repair made in ancient times on one of the frames towards the stern.

A very detailed analysis of a mass construction of warships is given by Tacitus (*Annals* II, 6), when he describes the building of the Germanicus fleet:

Rudder from the first Nemi ship, 39 AD.

Anchor from the first ship of Nemi, 39 AD. (Nemi, Museo delle Navi Romane, author's photographs, courtesy of the museum)

> It seemed that a thousand vessels were required, and they were speedily constructed, some of small draught with a narrow stem and stern and a broad centre, that they might bear the waves more easily; some flat-bottomed, that they might ground without being injured; several, furnished with a rudder at each end, so that by a sudden shifting of the oars they might be run into shore either way. Many were covered with decks, on which engines for missiles might be conveyed, and were also fit for the carrying of horses or supplies, and being equipped with sails as well as rapidly moved by oars, they assumed, through the enthusiasm of our soldiers, an imposing and formidable aspect.

In this important passage Tacitus attributes to Germanicus the invention of the double rudder, widely applied to river boats to facilitate route changing. It is exactly what we can see on one of Caligula's Nemi ships. This ship, the stem of which was identical to the stern so that their functions were interchangeable, had two pairs of rudders at the head. Also Seneca (*Letters*, LXXVI) recommends that a ship should be very stable (*stabilis*) and strong (*firma, solida*) with firmly connected joints (*iuncturae*) to make them watertight (*acquam excludentibus*), not easily giving way to the wind, and fast (*velox*). Ovid in his *Heroides* (XVI, 111 ff.) describes well the building of a fast ship made of oak, maybe a *liburna*: 'The oak is bent to build the frame for the speedy ship (*naves*), and the curving keel (*carina*) woven with ribbed sides. We add the pennons (*antennae*), and the sails (*velae*) hanging from the mast (*malo*)'.

The ship construction techniques were so good in the early Imperial age that it was possible to deliberately build a ship with defects, as in the plot of Emperor Nero against his mother Agrippina at Baia (59 AD). Anicetus, *Praefectus Classis Misenensis*, ordered that 'a vessel could be constructed, from which a part might by a contrivance be detached' (Tacitus, *Annales*, XIV, 3). The *triremis* upon which Agrippina embarked for Baia was composed

LEFT
Roman *oneraria*, from the mosaic of the Guildes, *c.* 122 AD. (Ostia, in situ, photograph courtesy of Domenico Carro)

RIGHT
A *scapha* full of soldiers, in a first-century fresco. Note the rectangular shield of the embarked soldiers, and the wide sail on the mast. (Pompeii, in situ, photograph courtesy of Domenico Carro)

Prow of the river ship *Alkedo*, 7 BC–15 AD. The small *Alkedo* has a prow fitted with a cutwater and a similar ram, what seems to be a miniature of the rams of the bigger warships of the period, particularly of the *liburnae*. (Pisa, Museum of the Roman Ships, photograph courtesy of Dr Andrea Camilli)

Relief of Roman *celox*, from Alba Fucens, second half of second century AD. The stern of this Roman warship has a high, up-curving and fan-shaped *aplustre* and in the space between there is always a small cabin for the captain or a centurion. Nearby are the ship's *vexilla*. The *celox* was a sort of speed *biremes*, at that time a sort of *liburna biremis*. (Cast of the Museo della Civiltà Romana, photo courtesy of Domenico Carro)

Fragment of the stempost of a warship with highly decorated *parasimon*, second century AD. The image of a marine *Triton* (sea divinity) and a small *amor* (*Eros*) brandishing a military flag decorate the port side of this ship. The ship's *parasimon* resembles that of the ships on Trajan's Column. Note the fragments of latticework screen. (Musée Carnavalet, Paris, photograph courtesy of Domenico Carro)

of a crew of selected marines. During the banquet with Nero other ships of the fleet damaged the *triremis*, and Agrippina was obliged to embark on the prepared ship. During the night, in the ship's cabin where Agrippina was resting, the ceiling, loaded with a great quantity of lead, collapsed and killed one of her attendants. Agrippina escaped by swimming to the coast, while another of her attendants, a woman called Acerronia, was killed with poles and oars when already in the sea, because she was claiming to be Agrippina. In the end Anicetus surrounded the villa of Antium where Agrippina was taking refuge, and slaughtered her and all her slaves. She was stabbed with a dagger by the *Praefectus* himself, the *trierarchus* Herculeius and Obaritus, a *centurion* of the marines (Tacitus. XIV, 8).

Local fleets were built in accordance with local styles and traditions. During the revolt of Anicetus, in 69 AD, the rebels concentrated all their warships (*camarae*) in Trabzon, the construction system of which was probably an evolution of a way of building already used there. The ships had a low freeboard but were broad of beam, and were fastened together without bronze or iron spikes. Tacitus records that in the area of Pontus 'When the sea is rough the sailors build up the bulwarks with planks (*tabulae*) to match the height of the waves, until they close in the hull like the roof of a house. Thus protected these vessels roll about amid the waves. They have a prow (*prora*) at both ends and their arrangement of oars may be shifted, so that they can be safely propelled in either direction at will'. In Byzantium, according to Cassius Dio (LXXV, 12), the ships were built by using timbers taken from the houses and braided ropes were made from the hair of the Byzantine women.

Armament and decoration

The names of the ships, mainly known from the epigraphic and papyrologic sources, were derived from those of the gods or mythological heroes (for example, *Castor*, *Mars* and *Danae* were all *triremis* of the Ravenna fleet in the second and third centuries AD), or from virtues typical of the Roman world (*triremis Providentia*, *Victoria* and *Pietas* of the Ravenna fleet), or from attributes of weapons (*Galeata*) and of the sea (*triremis Pinnata*, Ravenna fleet, first century AD). The small ship *Alkedo* (seagull) had its name incised on the bank of rowers. Sometimes the name was reflected in the *parasimon* of the ship, which formed the main decoration of the prow: on Trajan's flagship – a *triremis* of the Ravenna fleet represented on the Trajan Column – the *parasimon* is a seahorse. Images of the gods protecting the ships (*tutela*) were positioned on the prow and sculpted in ivory (Seneca, *Letters*, LXXVI), or painted on the stern

(Ovid, *Heroides*, XVI, 114): 'the hook-shaped stern (*puppis adunca*), too, received the painted gods'; (see also *Tristia*, IV, 6). The stern of Ovid's ship (*Tristia*, X, 1–2) was apparently adorned with a figure of Minerva clad in armour and took the name from the helmet of the goddess. Such a figure was called a *tutela*, a protecting emblem.

The armament of the ships of the Imperial navy was consistently the same as that of the Republican age, but the Roman naval architects introduced significant changes to warship design, one of which was related to the shape of the main ship's weapon, the ramming beak, the *rostrum*. The three-pronged ram of the Hellenistic age is still visible on the ships of the first century AD, but slowly it was dispensed with in favour of a single ram made of robust timber, similar to those of the ancient Phoenician warships. This massive horizontal timber was held in place by diagonals running back to the bow and vertically by a brace sloping up to the stem, and, from below, by the keel piece. Other timbers filled the gaps and the entire construction was sheathed in tightly fitting bronze casting ('brass-beaked ships of war', Seneca, *De Beneficiis*, XX). This kind of ram, rather than opening the timbers of the enemy's ship, was designed to spring them apart, and this explains the very sharp shape of the beak, visible for example on the ships on Trajan's Column. The bronze ram was often silvered or gilded (Seneca, *Letters*, LXXVI).

Beside the ram, the main weapons on warships were the artillery pieces (*tormenta*) mounted on the decks and the turrets. *Balistae*, scorpions and catapults are mentioned in the sources, but a new kind of throwing machine was also developed at the turn of the first century AD. They had their torsion springs made in all-metal mountings covered by protective cylinders, firmly held by a metal frame. They were ideal for warships, and so replaced the heavier types on larger warships as well as being fitted on the smaller ships which could not mount the older heavier artillery pieces.

Wooden pulleys and deadeyes regulated the movement of the sails through ropes made of sparto or hemp, as fragments from Comacchio and Pisa's vessels show clearly. As in the Consular age, a mast carrying a single square sail was positioned at the centre of the ship, supplemented by the *artemon*, the bowspritsail adopted from merchant

Fast Roman warships (*biremes liburnicae*), stucco frieze from the male *tepidarium* of the Terme Stabiane. On the prow of the upper and better preserved warship is a ram of the new typology. The second warship is shown at sea, and the double complement of oars is clearly visible. (Pompeii, first century AD, in situ, photographs courtesy of Domenico Carro)

Marble sculpture of ram (*rostrum*) first century AD. This decorated Imperial ram is 60cm long and it is thought to be an exact copy of an original in bronze. It has similar dimensions to the *rostrum* of a small *liburna*. Note the vertical and horizontal blades used to cut deeply into the hull of the enemy's ships. (Ostia, photograph courtesy of Domenico Carro)

Stone sculpture of *Rostrata*, first century AD. This artwork shows the front of a warship of the *Classis Ravennatis*, which had a naval squadron in Aquileia. As in earlier ages, the point approximately half way up to the stempost where the central wale timbers met was usually shaped as a secondary ram (*proembolion*), sometimes terminating in an animal head. (Aquileia, National Archaeological Museum, Author's photograph, courtesy of the museum)

Roman wooden anchor, second century AD. (Narbonne, Archaeological Museum, author's photograph, courtesy of the museum)

ships and mainly used to help in the steering of the vessel.

The ships were provided with two kinds of anchors. The first was a wooden one, complete with lead stock and hanging rope. One of the anchors from the Nemi galley, which can give an idea of the size of the warship, is 5.5m long, excluding the rope. It was made of oak spindle and flukes, linked by tenons and belaying pins. The hawsers were perfectly preserved. Each fluke edge was covered with iron nails, while the anchor stalk was leaden. Similar specimens have been found in Sardinia, Cartagena and Cagliari and in various other provinces. A big wooden anchor, decorated on the shaft with heart-shaped leaves in relief and similar to the sizes of the Nemi anchor, has been recovered from the merchant ship of San Rossore (Pisa), which has been dated to about 7 BC.

The second kind of Roman anchor was iron, a mobile block with the spindle and the flukes covered with wood, where the wooden covering (three pieces linked with tenons) might have had the function to widen the surface of the base or to cushion the impact against the keel, when the anchor was cast or set out. The finding of these iron specimens has allowed archeologists to date them to the Roman age. In recent history anchors with a mobile block were only invented in the 19th century by the Royal Navy. Simpler iron and stone anchors have been found in San Rossore, which date to the first and second century AD.

The Emperor's ships were heavily and luxuriously decorated: the *Liburnicae Deceres* of Caligula had sterns set with gems (*gemmatae puppae*), particoloured sails (*versicolora vela*), huge spacious baths, colonnades, and banquet halls, and even a great variety of vines and fruit trees. The ships had beautiful bronze protomes decorated with longitudinal and transversal structures, and those of the Nemi ships had the heads of lions, wolves and panthers, and the beautiful head of the Gorgon, Medusa, positioned high up. The lion at the end of the rudder stock completed the ornamental patterns on warships, as it was on one of Nemi's ships and as often represented in the iconography.

Wooden scoop from the Comacchio ship, 21 BC. The wooden scoop, or *sassola*, was used to bail out water that got inside the ship. (Comacchio Museum, photograph courtesy of Dr Cezary Wyszynski and Dr Fede Berti)

The ships were variously painted. According to Seneca (*Letters*, 6) and confirmed by the iconography, there were ships painted with precious colours. Ovid (*Heroides*, V, 65) speaks of prows (*prorae*), painted in purple. Blue was used on many naval ships for camouflage reasons. The colour is quite visible on the hulls of ships in Pompeiian frescoes. Other colours were used to on different parts of the vessels, although it is clear from iconography elsewhere that some parts were left in their natural wood. Pliny the Elder explains the technique for painting the warships (HN, XXXV, 41, 149): 'In ancient times there were but two methods of encaustic painting, in wax and on ivory, with the cestrum or pointed graver. When, however, this art came to be applied to the painting of ships of war (*classes*), a third method was adopted, that of melting the wax colours and laying them on with a brush, while hot. Painting of this nature, applied to vessels, will never spoil from the action of the sun, winds, or salt water.'

The contents of the Nemi, San Rossore and Comacchio ships, as well as those of many other shipwrecks, can give an idea of the kind of objects used on Roman warships: bronze balances with three gradations of weight, blocks used as moorage, a water wheel used for collecting water from the bilge, a piston-driven pump (like those found in Silchester), pieces of scuppers for draining water, boat hooks, baskets and nets, and other leather and wooden objects.

According to Quintus Ennius Palemo, a Roman erudite of the first century AD, the unit of measurement used to gauge the ship's tonnage was the *anfora*, which equated to 26.2 litres. Pelemo's particular *anfora* was consecrated and kept in the temple of Jupiter Capitolinus in Rome.

Part of a marine's leather *subarmale* from the Augustean levels of the San Rossore ships, 21–7 BC. (Pisa, Museum of the Roman Ships, photograph courtesy of Dr Andrea Camilli)

FIGHTING ON THE SEA: ROMAN NAVAL TACTICS IN THE EARLY EMPIRE

The Romans had a different attitude to naval warfare to their Greek forerunners, which was based on the efficient use of the discipline and power of their soldiery at sea. Marines and boarding tactics were the most important. The basic strategy of the Roman navy was to bring its ships in close to the enemy vessels so that the superior fighting abilities of the Roman troops could prevail. For this reason, the main tactics were to ram the enemy's hulls with the *rostrum* and, if necessary, the armed *classiarii* would board the ship.

The terrible effect of a Roman naval attack, the battle between the fleet of Septimius Severus and Byzantine ships in 192 AD, is described by Cassius Dio:

> ... when they had laden their boats with even more than these could bear, set sail, after waiting this time also for a great storm ... the Romans, observing that their vessels were overheavy and weighted down almost to the water's edge, put out against them. So they fell upon the craft, which were scattered about as wind and wave carried them, and what followed was anything but a naval battle; for they simply battered the enemy's boats mercilessly, thrusting at many of them with their boat-hooks, ripping many open with their beaks, and even capsizing some by their mere onset. The people in the boats were unable to do anything ... they would either be sunk by the force of the wind, to which they spread their sails to the full, or else would be overtaken by the enemy and destroyed.

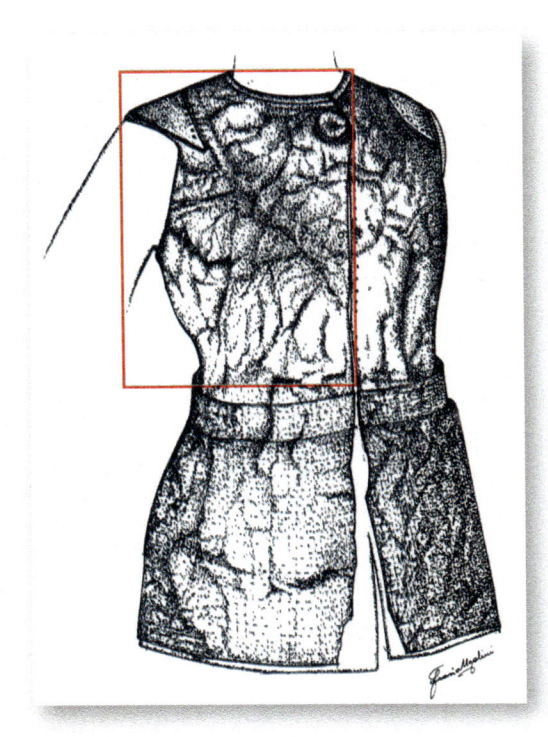

Attempt at a reconstruction of the leather *subarmale*. (Image courtesy of Dr Andrea Camilli)

For the best result, the Roman crews needed to be highly trained and drilled. Both at sea and in harbour the crews learned to row in unison, shipping oars, backing water and so on. Regular practice in large squadrons of ships was necessary to perfect battle manoeuvres.

However, during a naval battle, the most damage was done by the *tormenta*, an artillery piece that was sited on deck. A particular technique of late second-century naval warfare used against the Byzantines, the inhabitants of the Greek city of Byzantium, which was subject to Roman rule, is described by Cassius Dio (LXXV, 12):

> They used to capture not only ships that were sailing past, by making opportune attacks, but also triremes that were in their opponents' roads. They accomplished this by causing divers to cut their anchors under water and drive in the ships' sides nails that were attached by ropes to the friendly shore; then they would draw the ships towards them, so that these appeared to be sailing up all by themselves, of their own accord, with neither oarsman nor wind to urge them forward.

H **47 AD: GNAEUS DOMITIUS CORBULO SUBDUES THE CHAUCI**
According to Tacitus (*Annals*, XI, 18), the Chauci, under the leadership of Gannascus – a Canninefate who had been in Roman service – with an enterprising pirate fleet of light vessels ravaged the coast of Gaul. In order to engage the pirate fleet, Corbulo brought his triremes along the Rhine and the rest of his ships, depending on their draughts, by estuaries and canals. He then attacked and sunk the enemy boats. Here a Roman *triremis*, copied from the fresco of the *Aula Isiaca* in Pompeii, is ramming a light Germanic vessel, supported by a second Roman *triemiolia*. The ships, according to such iconography, had a waist-high bulwark, which stopped short of the bow structure, to give access to the *pàrodos*. The two *epotìdes* of the ships seem to emerge through the lower part of the oarboxes, forming two levels. The upper part of the oarbox probably served as a ventilation course as it is also visible on the Palazzo Spada relief. The top surface of the oarbox could serve as a *pàrodos*. The commodious stern shelter on each ship resembles those on the ships on Trajan's Column, but their oar systems are identical to old Republican models.

SELECT BIBLIOGRAPHY

Ancient Roman sources

Arrian, *Circumnavigation of the Black Sea*, (Circum.) ed. by Liddle. A., Bristol, 2003

Aulus Gellius - *Attic Nights* – *Noctes Atticae* (*Noct. Att.*) Latin text and English translation by J.C. Rolfe in Aulus Gellius: Volume II, Books 6–13, Loeb Classical Library, London, 1927

Caesaris Augusti Res Gestae et fragmenta, ed. Rogers R.S., Scott K., Word M.M., Benario H. W., Wayne State University Press, 1990

Cassius Dio, *Roman History – Romaika (Rom.)* translation by Cary E., Greek and English text in Loeb Classical Library, 9 vols, Harvard University Press, 1914–1927

Corpus Inscriptionum Latinorum (CIL), Consilio et Auctoritate Academiae Litterarum (Scientiarum) Regiae Borussicae (Germanicae), apud Georgium Reimerum (Gualterus de Gruyter), Berolini, 17 vol. in 73 tomes, Berolini (Berlin), 1869–1987

Florus, *Epitome of Roman History– Epitome de T. Livio Bellorum Omnium Annorum DCC Libri Duo (Epit.)*, Latin and English text in Loeb Classical Library, translation by E.S. Forster, Harvard University Press, 1984

Herodian, *History of the Empire from the Time of Marcus Aurelius – Herodiani Historiae a Marci - Principatu* – Ηρωδιανου μετα της Μαρκον Βασιλειας ιστοριας Greek and English text in Loeb Classical Library, *Herodian, History of the Empire, Books I–IV*, English translation by E.C. Echols Harvard University Press, 1961

Josephus, *Jewish Antiquities,* English texts in *The Works of Josephus*, translation by William Whiston, Peabody, 1987

Lucian, I, translation by A.M.Harmon, Greek and English text in Loeb Classical Library, Harvard University Press, 1971

Ovidius, *Heroides, Amores*, translation by Heinemann W., Greek and English text in Loeb Classical Library, Harvard University Press, 1914

Ovidius, *Tristia, Ex Ponto*, translation by A.L.Wheeler, Greek and English text in Loeb Classical Library, Harvard University Press, 1939

Palaemon, Quintus Rhemnius, Versi latini di Q. Rennio Fannio Palemone sopra i pesi e le misure dei Romani, in Sopra Guido d'Arezzo, dissertazione di L. Angeloni. Versi latini sopra i pesi e le misure, di Q.F.Palemone, Paris, 1811

Pliny the Elder, *Natural History – Historia Naturalis* (HN) Latin and English text in Loeb Classical Library, translation by H. Rackham 10 vols, Harvard University Press, 1938–1962

Propertius, *The poems of Sextus Propertius*, ed. McCulloch, J.P., Los Angeles-London, 1972

Seneca, *On benefits (the complete works of Lucius Annaeus Seneca)*, University of Chicago Press, 2010

Seneca, *Ad Lucilium, epistulae morales*, ed. Capps E., Page T.E., Rouse W.H.D., translation by R. M. Gummere, Loeb Classical Library, III vol., Harvard University Press, 1920

Seneca, *Letters from a Stoic*, translation by R. M. Gummere, Loeb Classical Library, Harvard University press, 1925

Suetonius (Suet.) *The Twelve Caesars – De Vita Caesarum, Augustus* (*Aug.*); *Caligula* (Gajus); *Claudius* (*Claud.*); *Galba*; *Nero;* Latin and English text in *The lives of the Caesars, Suetonius,* 2 vols., Loeb Classical Library, translation by J.C.Rolfe, Harvard University Press, 1914

Tacitus *Annals – Annales (Ann.)* Latin and English text in *Tacitus IV-V, Annals 4–6, 11–12, 13–16*, translation by J. Jackson, Loeb Classical Library, Harvard University Press, 1937

Tacitus, *The Histories – Historiae (Hist.) Tacitus II, Histories 1–3*, translation by C.H. Moore, Loeb Classical Library, Harvard University Press, 1925; *Tacitus III, Histories 4–5, Annals 1–3*, Loeb Classical Library, Harvard University Press, 1931, translation by C.H. Moore and J. Jackson

Tacitus I, Agricola. Germania. Dialogue on Oratory, translation by M. Hutton and W. Peterson, Loeb Classical Library, Harvard University Press, 1914;

Scholarship

Academia Scientiarum socialium et politicarum dacoromana, *Inscriptiones Daciae et Scythiae Minoris Antiquae – Inscriptiones Daciae Romanae*, vol. I-III.4, ed. Pascu S., Russu I.I., Florescu G., Petolescu C.C., Bucarest, 1975-1988

Bonino, M., *Un sogno ellenistico, le navi di Nemi*, Pisa, 2013

Campbell, B., *War and society in Imperial Rome, 31BC–AD 284*, London-New York, 2002

Casson, L., *Ships and seamanship in the ancient world*, Princeton University Press, 1971

Carro, D., 'Le grandi coalizioni marittime nell'arcipelago, in *Classica, Storia della marina di Roma, Testimonianze dell'antichità*, nr. I, Roma, 1994

Carro, D., 'Pompeo Magno e il dominio del mare', in *Classica, Storia della marina di Roma, Testimonianze dell'antichità*, nr. VI, Roma, 1997

Carro, D., 'Appendici Marittime, in *Classica, Storia della marina di Roma, Testimonianze dell'antichità*, nr. XI, Roma, 2002

Cervellati, N., *I diplomi militari : una fonte epigrafica ufficiale per lo studio delle flotte provinciali romane*, tesi di dottorato, Bologna, 2009

D'Amato, R., *Imperial Roman Naval Forces 31 BC–AD 500*, Oxford, 2009

Daremberg-Saglio, *Dictionnaire des Antiquités Grecques et Romaines*, Paris, 1877–1919

Fede Berti, *Fortuna Maris, la nave romana di Comacchio*, Bologna, 1990

Henniquiau, M., - Martin, J., *La Marine Antique (2)*, Pantin, 1999

Konen, H.C., *Classis Germanica*, St. Katharinen, 2001

Mason, D.J.P., *Roman Britain and the Roman navy*, Stroud, 2003

Morrison, J. S. & Gardiner, R. (ed.), *The Age of the Galley: Mediterranean Oared Vessels Since Pre-Classical Times*. Conway Maritime, London, 1995

Morrison, J. S. & Coates, J.F., *Greek and Roman oared warships*. Oxford, 1996

Murray, W. M., *Recovering rams from the battle of Actium. Experimental Archaeology in Nicopolis*, in Proceedings of 2 International Nicopolis Symposium 11-15 September 2002, Preveza, 2007, 445-451, figs. 333-341

Pavis d'Escurac, H., *Reflexions sur la classis Africana Commodiana*, in: *Melanges d'histoire ancienne offerts à William Seston*, Paris 1974, 397-408

Pitassi, M, *The navies of Rome*, Chippenham and Eastbourne, 2009

M. Reddé, *Mare Nostrum: les infrastructures, le dispositif et l'histoire de la marine militaire sous l'empire romain* (Bibliothéque des Écoles françaises d'Athènes et de Rome CCLX), Rome, 1986

Speidel, M.A., *The development of the Roman Forces in Northeastern Anatolia, new evidences for the history of the Exercitus Cappadocicus*, in Herr unr Herrschaft im Romischen Reich der Hoen Kaiserzeit, Stuttgart, 2009, 595-631

Starr, C. G. *The Roman Imperial Navy, 31 B. C.–A. D. 324*, Chicago, 1993

Various, *The ancient ships of Pisa*, New York, 2001

Viereck H. D. L, *Die römische Flotte, Classis Romana*, Hamburg, 1996

INDEX

References to illustrations are shown in **bold**

actuaria 35–36, **37** (36)
Agricola 24
Agrippa 7
Agrippina 39–40
Albintimilium 9
Alexandria 19, 23
Alkedo **37** (36), 38, **39**, 40
Anatolia 24
anchors **38**, **42**, **42**
Anicetus 39, 40
armament **41**, 41–42, 44
Arno, river 27
Artabanus, King 14–15
artemon 41–42
artillery 41, 44
Augustus, Emperor 4–5, **15**, 19, 23
Aulus Gellius 26–27
Aurelius, Marcus 11, 14, 23
  Column 27, **27**, 36

Barbarians 14, 15, **21** (20)
Batavians 10, **13** (12)
Bedriacum, battle of (69 AD) 9–10
Bellum Germanicum et Sarmaticum (168–180 AD) 14
biremes **17** (16), **25** (24), 26, 28, 34, 40, 41
Black Sea 24
boat sheds **30**, 31
boats 27–28
bridge-building 27–28
Britain, invasion of 22
bulwarks **11**, **31**, 32, 34, **34**, 38, 40, **45** (44)
Burdo, Julius
Byzantium 10, 11–12, 40, 44

Caesar, Julius 5, 22
Caligula, Emperor 22, 23, 34–35, 42
cargo carriers 7, 14, 36, **39**
'Carthaginian ship' **9**, 32
carvel shipbuilding method 36
Cassius Dio 27–28, 40, 44
celox **21** (20), 40
Cerialis 10
Chauci **45** (44)
civil wars 5, 8–10
Civilis, Gaius Julius 10, 27
Claudius 15, 18, 22, 23, 24, 35
Clemens, Suedius 8
Comacchio ship 41,43, **43**
commanders of fleets 15–16
construction of ships 36, 38–40
Corbulo, Gnaeus Domitius 30, **45** (44)
crew members 15–16
  see also oarsmen
Ctesiphon 14–15
Cyzicus 24

Dacia, Conquest of (101–106 AD) 11, 12, 14, **15**, **17** (16), **19**, **20**, 34, 35
Danube, river 11, 12, 14, **17** (16), 20, **20**, **21** (20), 22, 27
deceres 34–35, 42
decks 9, **11**, **13** (12), 30, 32, 34, **37** (36)
decoration of ships **17** (16), 40–43
dimensions of ships 27, **37** (36), 38
Domitian, Emperor 11, 22
Drusus the Elder 19

Egypt 19, 23
epotis 30, **31**, 34, **45** (44)
equipment 43
Euphrates, river 14
exploratory ships **33** (32)

flagships 8, 10, **15**, **16**, **17** (16), 18, 26, 28, 40
fleets (*classes*)
  Africana Commodiana 23
  Alexandrina 15, 16, 23
  Arabica 23
  Britannica **13** (12), 14, 22, **22**, 24, 28
  Forum Julii 26
  Germanica 8, 10, **13** (12), 19, 20, 28, 38–39
  Mesopotamica 12, 23
  Misenensis 5, 8, **8**, **10**, 11, **11**, **12**, 15, 18–19, 23, **30**, 30–31, 39
  Moesica 12, 14, 20, 22, 28
  Nova Libica 23–24
  Pannonica 14, **17** (16), 20, **21** (20), 22, 28
  Pontica 10, 24
  Praetoriae 5, 9, 12, 14, 18, 19, 23, 31, 34
  Ravennatis 5, 11, 15, 18–19, **19**, 26, 40, **42**
  Rhine 10, 19–20, 28, 30
  Syriaca 12, 23–24
  provincial 15, 19, 20, 22, 23
  hierarchy of 15–16
  organisation of 15–16
  size 5
Florus 19
Forum Julii 5, 8, 15
Fossa Drusiana 19–20
Fucine lake 24, 26

Gaul 5, 8
Ghyteion model 34, **34**
gods, decorations of 40–41
gubernator 16

harbours 5, 15, 18, 22
Herodian 14–15
hexeris ('Sixes') 18, 26, 34–35, **37** (36)
hulls 30, **35**, 35, 36, 38, 40

Iazyges **21** (20)
Isis fresco 5, **6**, **9**, **10**, **11**

Könen, H.C. 23

latticework screens **13** (12), **17** (16), 28, 31–32, 34, **35**
liburna/liburnian **6**, **11**, **13** (12), 18, **18**, **19**, **22**, 24, 28, 32–34, **33** (32), **34**, **35**
  liburnica biremis 10, 12, **17** (16), **25** (24), 28, 34
  liburnicae deceres 34–35, 42

Marcomannic Wars 11, **21** (20), 24
Maturus, Marius 8
Mauretania 23, 24
Maximianus, Marcus Valerius 14
Mediterranean 5, 18, 23–24, 26
merchant ships 35–36, 42
Monumentum Ancyranum 5
Morrison, J.S. 26, 31, 32, **33** (32)

names of ships 40
Naumachia (mock naval battles) 9, 18, 24, **24**, 26
naves maioris formae 26
naves minoris formae 26
navy
  in the early empire 4–5, 8–12
  organization of 15–24
  see also fleets
Nemi ships 35, **35**, **36**, 38, **38**, 39, 42, 43
Nepos, Titus Fulvius 29
Nero, Emperor 15, 18, 24, 39–40
Niger, Pescennius 11

oar ports **25** (24), 28, **29** (28), 30, **31**, 38
oar systems **13** (12), **17** (16), **19**, **25** (24), 26, 28, **29** (28), 30–31, **30**, **31**, 32, **33** (32), 34, **34**, 38, 40, **41**, **45** (44)
oarsmen 16, **16**, **25** (24), 26, **26**, **29** (28), 30, 31, 44
Odysseus' ship **4**
officers 15–16
onerariae (cargo carriers) 7, 14, 36, **39**
Ops (flagship) 26
ornaments 36, 40–41, **42–43**
Ostia 18
Ostia relief **30**, 31
Otho, Emperor 8, 9–10
outriggers 31, 34, 35
Ovid 39, 41, 43

paintwork 32, **33** (32), **37** (36), 40–41, 43
Palemo, Quintus Ennius 43
Pannonia 14, 19
parasimon 30, **31**, 40, **40**
parodos **25** (24), **31**, 34, **45** (44)
Parthians 12, 14–15, 23, 24
Phoenician models 31
Pliny the Elder 43
polyremes 26
Pompeius, Sextus 5
pontoon bridges **27**, 27–28
Pozzuoli reliefs **8**, **28**, 30
Praetoria Triremis 28, 30
proembolion 30
proreta 16
prows 4, 35, 36, **39**, 40

quadriremes ('Fours') 18, 24, 26, **29** (28), 31–32
quinqiremes ('Fives') 18, **23**, 26, **29** (28), 30, 31–32, **31**, 32
rams 30, **31**, 34, **39**, 41, **41**, **42**, 44, **45** (44)
Ravenna harbour 5
Reddé, M. 23
rudders 11, **36**, **38**, **38**, 39

sails **13** (12), 27, **39**, 41
San Rossore ships 27, 42, 43, **43**
sassola 43
scaphae 27, **39**
Seleucia 23
Seneca 16, 39, 41, 43
Severus, Septimius 11, 12, 14–15, 44
shipbuilding 36, 38–40
skini 34
Starr, C.G. 22, 23
steering 35, 41–42
stemposts 5, **8**, **9**, **12**, 15, 18, 26, **29** (28), **30**, **31**, 32, **40**
sterns **16**, **18**, **28**, 30, 31–32, **40**, 41
subarmale 43, 44
Suetonius 22, 34

Tacitus 8, 9, 15, 24, 26, 28, 30, 35, 38–39, 40, **45** (44)
tactics 26, 43–44
Taurunum 11, 22
thalamites 30, 31
thranites 30, 31
throwing machines **37** (36), 41
Tiberius 20, 22
tormenta 44
Trabzon 24, 40
Trajan, Emperor 11, 12, 14, **16**, **17** (16), 23, 40
  Column 14, **15**, **19**, **20**, 27, 28, 31–32, 34, **34**, 35, **35**, 36, 38, 40, 41
Triremes ('Threes') 8, **17** (16), 18–19, **19**, **22**, 24, **25** (24), 26, 28, **28**, 30–31, 32, **45** (44)
troop transport ships 35–36, **37** (36)
tutela 40–41

Valens 9
ventilation **17** (16), **25** (24), 26, **31**, 32, 34, **45** (44)
Vespasian 10, 11, 22, 23
Viereck, H.D.L. **37** (36)
Vitellius, Emperor 8, 9–10

weapons **37** (36), **41**, 41–42, 44
  rams 30, **31**, 34, **39**, 41, **41**, **42**, 44, **45** (44)
wood, types of 38, 39

Year of the Four Emperors 8–12

zygites 30, 31